THE SERVE
KEY TO
WINNING
TENNIS

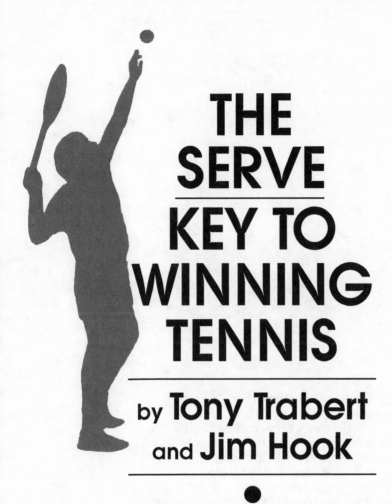

THE
SERVE
KEY TO
WINNING
TENNIS

by **Tony Trabert**
and **Jim Hook**

DODD, MEAD & COMPANY • NEW YORK

Published by Dodd, Mead & Company, Inc.
79 Madison Avenue, New York, N.Y. 10016
Distributed in Canada by
McClelland and Stewart Limited, Toronto
Manufactured in the United States of America
Designed by Michael Perpich
First Edition

Library of Congress Cataloging in Publication Data

Trabert, Tony.
   The serve.

   1. Tennis—Serve. I. Hook, Jim, 1912-   . II. Title.
GV1002.9.S47T73   1984   796.342'21   84-1510
ISBN 0-396-08298-X
ISBN 0-396-08299-8 (pbk.)

TO KATHY, BROOKE, AND MIKE

CONTENTS

Preface   ix

Introduction   xi

PART ONE • TENNIS AND THE SERVE

1. Tennis: Structural Wrinkles Often Overlooked. .   1
2. The Serve: Key to Winning Tennis   5
3. The Serve: Degree of Difficulty.   8
4. The Serve: Component Parts   10

PART TWO • THE SERVE: PREPARATORY MEASURES

5. Step One: The Grip (Racket)   17
6. Step Two: The Hold (Ball)   20
7. Step Three: The Decisions.   23
8. Step Four: The Target   26
9. Step Five: The Position (Base Line)   32
10. Step Six: The Stance   39

PART THREE • THE SERVE: PRELIMINARY MOTIONS

11. Step Seven: The Respiration.   47
12. Step Eight: The Lean.   50
13. Step Nine: The Bounce (Ball)   52
14. Step Ten: The Fingering (Ball)   54
15. Step Eleven: The Recovery.   56

PART FOUR • THE SERVE: PROPELLING ACTIONS

16. Step Twelve: The Lift (Ball) . . . .　63
17. Step Thirteen: The Swing/Strike/Swing . . . .　74
18. Step Fourteen: The Stride . . . .　102
19. Step Fifteen: The Finish . . . .　104

PART FIVE • THE SERVE: OTHER SIGNIFICANT
##　　　　　CONSIDERATIONS

20. The Serve: Doubles . . . .　111
21. The Serve: Tactical Maneuvers . . . .　118
22. The Serve: Coping with the Milieu . . . .　121
23. The Serve: Practice . . . .　127
24. Tennis: Choosing a Racket . . . .　131

Postscript . . . .　138

Preface

From what we have been able to gather, this is probably the only book in existence that limits its basic discussion solely to the tennis serve. Up to now, no one has evidently felt that the subject was comprehensive enough to warrant such treatment. This may be somewhat surprising to those who have come to recognize the importance of the service delivery to the successful tennis game.

That *The Serve: Key to Winning Tennis* has the dimension it does derives primarily from the fact that the great preponderance of its material is entirely fresh and original. Rest assured that what you will find in the following pages is far more than a humdrum compendium or rehash of the hackneyed and often confusing commentary on the subject, which is found in so many texts covering the general topic of tennis-playing skills. Rather, it is essentially a smorgasbord of information that offers both the new and more experienced player, in easily identifiable and well-defined portions, a wide choice of as much or as little of just about everything anybody would want to know about the key stroke in tennis—the serve. While the approach is detailed on occasion, and basically diagnostic, it has a light touch and puts particular emphasis on clarity of expression.

For the most part, the technical input originated in my corner and, in all cases, reflects my own theories on how best to serve a tennis ball. The analytical input, on the other hand, is principally the bailiwick of my coauthor, Jim Hook, a writer who has always loved the game and, over the years, developed some provocative thoughts as part of a unique curiosity about the structure of the service delivery and the relation of the serve and tennis, as a whole, to other sports.

With the writing completed, we'd be the first to admit, however, that it's pretty difficult to learn how to serve a tennis ball by simply reading a book and examining its drawings and photographs. To grasp the subject fully, scrutinizing the sedentary communication of printed material must be supplemented with studying the live action of an expert performance—be it a demonstration by a teaching professional or a match between top-notch contestants.

But the right words can get the beginner off in the right direction and pull the individual with the more finished game out of a bad rut.

We hope you will find them here.

Tony Trabert

On the court, in the TV booth, or via the printed page, Tony Trabert is as knowledgeable and articulate as the best on the subject about which he knows the most—tennis. You'll discover he's at his peak in *The Serve: Key to Winning Tennis*. It was a pleasure to work with him in this joint effort.

Several people deserve thanks for comments about the book's contents and assistance in making the project fly. These include Charlotte and Bill Kraft, Jack Kramer, Alex Kroll, Nancy Neeld, Alan Pope, Bill Talbert, and Ellsworth Vines. Particularly appreciated are the contributions of my indefatigable wife, Kathy, whose proofreading service was faultless (if you'll pardon the expression) and the several helpful suggestions of Tony's daughter, Brooke, and son, Mike—to all three of whom *The Serve: Key to Winning Tennis* is affectionately dedicated.

Jim Hook

Introduction

Tennis is challenging competition for some, good exercise for others, and a lot of fun for everyone—gal or guy, young or old. It's unfortunate that there seems to be such a diverging judgment and mixed opinion about which part of the game can do the most to make a player a winner.

Maybe it's the language.

Like no other sport, tennis does suffer from a strange, hand-me-down lingo that leaves much to be desired.

The term *love*, for instance, derives from *oeuf*, the French word for *egg*. While a convenient reference to the oval shape of the zero in tennis scoring it is intended to identify, the expression is certainly bizarre—to put it mildly.

According to Webster, the noun *rally* generally designates the act of "uniting vigorously in a common cause." It incurs a rather farfetched application, however, when employed to describe the "interchange of a series of strokes between players intent on winning a point"—the word's true lexicographical meaning in the tennis context, by the way, despite most racket buffs limiting its use to indicate practice or warm-up play.

Or take *volley*. Its root meaning specifies the flight of a missile that is generated by a propelling agency—normally from ground level. In the tennis vernacular, on the other hand, it describes the flight of a ball that can only be generated by a receiving agency—and always from a point above ground level.

Striker-out, an expression denoting the player who receives the serve, is a real loser. Its origin is obscure, its sense is unfathomable, and its use, fortunately, is limited and should eventually disappear from the tennis scene.

The verb *serve* could be the most misconstrued term of all. The dictionary insists that its use in tennis merely signifies the feat of "putting the ball in play"—an action mindful of what a referee does at the start of a basketball game. This perfunctory-sounding operation hardly fits the need to portray the most powerful and aggressive employment of offensive play performed in the entire game.

Be that as it may, it's hard to see how a downplay of emphasis in its definition can adequately explain why a random selection of twenty books on tennis instruction allocates an average of less than 12 percent of the pages in each to a discussion of the serve—in light of the fact that more points are won with this stroke than any other.

The Serve: Key to Winning Tennis is intended to remedy this unbalance. If we somewhat overcompensate in the process, we do so with open eyes and a firm convicton that it's high time the subject receive the attention it deserves.

The serve is the most difficult stroke in tennis to perform well because it is the most challenging one to teach properly, and it is the most challenging stroke to teach properly—and is often taught improperly—because the instructor simply does not fully perceive that the serve has many angles deserving far more attention than he is prepared to furnish the student. This would suggest, to a large degree, that the more precise the approach and systematized the pattern, the more adept that instruction can be.

As a consequence, in the chapters that follow: diction will, at times, be repetitive to stress vital points and help the reader retain them; long sentences will occasionally be used to establish and maintain continuity of thought where tangency of ideas is desirable; cross-references will frequently be cited to accentuate the close association between—if not actual integration of—a good number of the serve's elements which the book describes; and synonyms will rarely be substituted for key words, the object being to assure clarity of understanding and habituate employment of proper terminology. In addition, some of the things we plan to say will seem pretty obvious—particularly to those who have played tennis for some time and are, therefore, the very ones most likely to overlook the thought and attention these matters deserve.

Don't let it throw you—and we are especially addressing those readers who may be inclined to place appreciable emphasis on the simplistic.

We like to think our plan is all very much strategized—and for the good reason that our subject has many more angles deserving far more attention than generally recognized.

One other item.

This book has been written for men *and* women.

We hasten to stress this fact because its wording is, frankly, male oriented.

Rather than have us "he and/or she" the writing to death and drive our readers up the wall in the process, however, we ask you to acquiesce in this simple proposition: until our mother tongue develops an adequate neutral terminology that can accommodate both sexes, there is little purpose in fighting the truth that the masculine hold on much of our language has been strong for centuries and will probably continue to be so for some time to come.

Be honest, ladies.

What difference does it really make if our hypothetical tennis player is always referred to as "him"?

We think we have something to say.

A good bit of it is rather difficult to express in words.

Don't ask us to botch it up by insisting that we give equal time to both genders in our use of the personal pronoun.

Thirty and out.

PART ONE

TENNIS AND THE SERVE

1 Tennis: Structural Wrinkles Often Overlooked

Let's get things under way with some words about several peculiarities in the structure of tennis as a game.

There are facets about its fundamental character that the player may never have considered.

For a starter, focus for a moment on the different kinds of opposition with which a player must cope in several of our most popular sports.

In golf, contestants battle the course in the process of estimating distance, generating propulsion and controlling direction with maximum efficiency. Their battle with each other is purely psychological.

In bowling, contestants battle the alley and the pins in the process of providing spin and speed as well as controlling direction with maximum efficiency. Their battle with each other is again purely psychological.

But in tennis, contestants do direct battle with both the court and each other. Actually the intent is to beat the court first, but with just the right reduction in margin of error that will give the player the best chance in addition to beat his opponent by making it difficult—if not impossible—for that opponent to keep the ball in play.

Most team games (football, baseball, basketball, hockey, etc.) require contestants to do direct battle with the playing field and its trappings (goal posts, base lines, hoops, cages, etc.) as well as with the opposing players. Tennis, however, like any of the several games involving ball and racket, is just about unique in this regard as far as athletic sports are concerned where only two people need be the competitors. In almost all other so-called individual sports the mechanics of beating one's opponent relate solely to the necessity of adequately contending with the playing arena and its accompanying hazards and limitations. In tennis, the mechanics of adequately contending with the court, and its accompanying net hazard and line limitations, are only supplementary to the eventual necessity of directly beating one's opponent through patience, aggressiveness, or a combination of both.

The fact that a tennis player is directly battling both the court and his opponent makes each tennis shot doubly important. It further means that the ablest use of the most effective shot—the serve—will furnish the biggest payoff.

The truth should be obvious.

Learn to serve well early in your tennis career and you will gain a tremendous advantage over the player who does not.

Looking at the athletic spectrum from an entirely different point of view, there are two types of competitive sports.

In the first category are those sports whose playing time involves a series of successive episodes, where action for each episode is initiated from rest by one of the contestants. As a general rule, *episodic* sports include all competitive sports other than those involved with racing against the clock or contending with some other device that gauges human effort or capacity.

In the second category are those sports whose playing time is continuous from start to finish. These include cycling, foot running, motoring, sailing, skiing, swimming, track, or any kind of competition requiring man-made or man-guided motivation to minimize time, maximize distance, etc.

The options afforded the contestants' initiating action in an episodic sport can be many or few. In the main, they tend to be more numerous and complex in team sports than in individual sports.

Take baseball for example.

The pitcher on the mound starts an episode each time he throws to the batter. Before doing so, however, he must determine the speed, spin, and target for the upcoming delivery to the plate—the selection being dependent on such variables as who the batter is, who is on base, who is up next, how many are out, what the score is, what inning it is, what pitch the catcher asks for, etc.

Or take football.

The quarterback with the ball starts an episode each time he calls for a center snap. Before the ball is moved, however, he must determine for the ensuing play how the offensive formation will be set up and the ball advanced (run, pass, or kick)—the selection being dependent on such variables as the relative strengths and weaknesses of the competing teams, the position of the ball on the field, the score, the amount of time left in the game, etc.

On the other hand there is basically a single best way under a given set of conditions to hit a ball in golf or roll a ball in bowling. While all involve individual sports that are episodic, the object of each of these actions is to groove and maintain a fundamentally facsimile operation rather than devise a change of pace to keep the opposition guessing.

Tennis is one of the few episodic sports requiring only two competitors where the initiator (the server) must select one of several different courses of action—each of which merits consideration.

For example, where the golfer has only one preferred target at the beginning of an episode—be it fairway, green, or pin—and one preferred way to get there—granted the high or low fade or draw selected may be contingent on the weather, or state of the course— the tennis server must choose from a number of commensurate alternatives in planning a service delivery. His decision on how and where to direct the ball not only depends on light, sun, wind, and the type of court surface on which the match is being played, but also such additional variables as the point, game, and set score, the condition of the tennis balls and, most important, the strengths and weaknesses of the players involved.

The need to weigh these several options sees tennis serving relying to a surprising degree on strategy rather than almost solely on athletic skills, as is the case in such *go, no go* sports as golf or bowling, where room for maneuvering the propelling techniques is pretty limited—if existent at all. And that strategy in tennis can best be generated if the serve is so prepared, so structured, and so performed that it is key to calling the play best suited for the occasion, i.e., that it actually quarterbacks a winning tennis offense.

When native or physical ability comes up short, flexibility in the choice of service may not make tennis a better game for the amateur than the other two.

But it can make it more fun for more people.

This is particularly true for the older but experienced weekend player with a good serve who finds it possible to compete favorably with younger players, even when the age differential measures as much as ten to fifteen years.

Once again the message is there for the listening.

Polish up your serve. Make it an effective working tool, and tennis will continue to be a sport you can play with surprisingly good results for a long time.

2 The Serve: Key to Winning Tennis

Every competitive sport involves a key skill that must be developed to permit successful play.

In golf it is putting.

In bowling it is lifting.

And in tennis it is serving.

Unfortunately, in too many cases beginners are not immediately aware that this is so. This occurs because the majority of teachers—both professional and amateur—tend to spend an inordinate amount of time and effort at the start drilling pupils on other features which—while essential to the generation of the complete player—do not merit primary attention during the early lessons.

Take golf for example.

Who ever heard of conducting a first golf lesson on a putting green?

It just doesn't happen.

With rare exception, the teaching pro starts off showing the novice the preferred club grip for hitting through the ball, the right stance at address, and the correct swing. Throughout the course of instruction, about 90 percent of the professional's time is devoted to developing know-how in these areas. The other 10 percent is available for other matters—including how to putt. This lack of attention ignores the fact that over half of the stroke differential in a golf match between players of equal ability normally takes place on the green.

Actually many golf tutors brush off the need for extensive putting instruction with the rather vague excuse that putting is basically an individual technique that each player must develop for himself; that the important thing is to be comfortable and relaxed so that the player can devise, through trial and error, that modus operandi that suits him best.

A somewhat comparable situation exists in bowling.

The beginner at tenpins, for example, is frequently too intent on grappling with such questions as, "How many steps should I take?" or "Should I keep my eyes on an alley spot or a pin when I release the ball?" to recognize the vital significance of employing the appropriate lift in controlling direction and spin. Furthermore, few bowling instructors spend sufficient time getting this point across at the time instruction begins. As a consequence, many pupils have difficulty fitting it in later when bad habits have already been firmly established.

In large measure, modern teaching methods suffer the same sort of failings in properly determining how an individual should be introduced to the game of tennis.

More often than not, attention is first directed to the preferred grip for hitting ground strokes.

Next, the pupil is asked to swing his racket in conjunction with a proper stance, a proper shift of body weight, and a proper follow-through with forehand and backhand.

After a brief session of going through a series of dummy motions that see the pupil merely fanning the air with his racket, the inevitable bucket of balls appears, and the first practice sessions get under way on a court—with the teacher feeding easy shots for the pupil to return as best he can. This latter exercise may continue, with a few modifications, throughout the entire sequence of lessons. And the fact that it is exercise and manages to introduce the pupil to the game's *cross net action* early in his instruction is admittedly a sound reason for breaking him in via this approach. Unfortunately, as a consequence, meaningful emphasis on the tennis serve—if it takes place at all—occurs, in most instances, late in the learner's schooling.

This lack of attention—normally little, mostly late, often both—is unfortunate, to say the least. It neglects the importance of the one stroke that should be—and can be—far and away the most valuable weapon in a tennis player's arsenal. Out-and-out untouchable winners (*aces*), forced errors, and weak service returns that are easy to put away mean the serve can be responsible for more than half of the points in a competition between evenly matched contestants.

The situation is made even worse when the tennis instructor takes the same kind of position on serving that many golf teachers do on putting, i.e., that while there are a few fundamentals a player must learn about striking the ball, the final determination of how he can serve best is an individually developed skill, which is primarily dependent on, and therefore closely tailored to, such variables as his height, build, strength, coordination, age, etc.

The result is a majority of participants in the game of tennis serve improperly.

Given x number of players selected at random from a group with something less than average ability, one can expect to find close to x number of serving styles. Only the various individual interpretations of the artistry demanded by today's popular dance routines can come close to competing in a count of diverse techniques. Both conditions exist principally for the same reason: lack of instruction.

Of course as far as disco steps are concerned, concentrating attention on execution can be self-defeating if it encroaches too severely on the ego trip of the current revved-up creative "ballroom" artist, intent on doing his thing—and only his thing. No such hit-or-miss methods have a place in tennis, however. The skill involved in properly serving a tennis ball can rarely be programmed by an individual without a substantial recognition of and appreciation for the elements contained in its optimum construction.

We hope this book can stimulate that understanding.

3 The Serve: Degree of Difficulty

To serve well in tennis is not easy.

It's not uncommonly difficult either as long as the player understands what service choices are available within the confines of his own limitations, selects the option that seems best at the moment, and concentrates on bringing it off.

The total service action is a surprisingly lengthy one, comprising, as it does, a series of steps which must always be fitted together in the same ordered pattern to yield the best results. Executing this same routine every time the serve is made demands a good deal of attention, patience, and perseverance. If one includes all the preparatory measures and preliminary motions—as well as the actual propelling actions—each separate service delivery should take approximately five to ten seconds.

Tennis serving has more diverse elements requiring more coordination and inviting more error than most actions in athletic sports.

In golf, the ball is at least stationary when struck.

In bowling, the pins are not only stationary when struck, but the movement toward release of the ball is in one plane and, with the exception of the windup swing of the propelling arm, in one direction.

But in the tennis serve the ball is in motion when struck, the movement toward striking the ball can be in several planes and in many directions, and the body and all of its extremities rise, fall, swivel, and bend in a multiplicity of varied movements—a good many of them simultaneous.

While serving involves a number of individual steps and a variety of elements that necessitate appreciable synchronization, it is not as formidable as it may sound.

No acrobatics are required.

No excessively punishing strain on the body's muscles occurs.

No unduly enervating drain on the cardiovascular system takes place.

With tennis a rather strenuous sport in the overall, however, problems can arise when a long match brings on fatigue, and the body cries out for compromise of an otherwise acceptable regimen. The serving arm gets a little heavy, the legs lose some of their resilience, and the breathing quickens. But, worst of all, the mind gets restless and is apt to wander from the task at hand in the course of accepting shortcuts in the service action's prescribed modus operandi.

When these difficulties are compounded by the vicissitudes of the natural elements—a strong or gusty wind, intermittent sun and clouds, a hot, humid day—it demands more than a modest amount of tenacity to sustain a high level of service performance.

Even those with great natural ability discover that time and effort are required to groove the complete serve into a reasonably consistent configuration. What is more, it calls for appreciable personal discipline from any player to form the habit of using the knowledge of what he can do with a serve to plan what he should do, and most important, to train himself to think hard about what he will try to do just prior to initiating the final propelling actions. Our advice: unless these several physical and mental acts can eventually be performed in a relatively comfortable and relaxed way, without creating tensions that can make serving more a chore than a pleasure, it's possible that tennis is not your game.

Some other recreation may be more fun.

After all, that's what sports should be all about.

4 The Serve: Component Parts

When two tennis opponents of roughly equal ability play together for the first time, each normally delays estimating his chances of winning until he has received the other's service. And often the player with better skills in other areas of the game ends up the loser, because the man across the net has the better serve. That this should ever happen is unfortunate—and, in most cases, unnecessary.

Of course, no two people ever serve exactly the same way. Dissimilarities in skeletal construction, raw physical talent, mental approach, and, most important, instinctive athletic tempo and rhythm, while not actually controlling, always modify the final product to some degree.

Nor is it vital that everyone try to serve exactly the same way. This could be as frustrating and wasteful as insisting on wearing a good-looking jacket because it is so chic, despite the fact that it doesn't fit.

But all tennis players should think through the tennis serving procedure from start to finish. This is as true for the beginner as for the individual who has played the game for a number of years and picked up some quirks in his service delivery which he wishes to iron out—if not entirely discard.

The rest of this book is devoted for the most part to an explanation of how a tennis player can break down the tennis serving procedure into its component parts and, in the process, actually teach himself the fundamentals of the serve or give himself a fresh point of view on service delivery particulars. The basic orientation is directed toward the singles player. The several modifications in technique required in doubles play are discussed in Chapter 20.

As we see it, there are as many as fifteen steps that can be involved in the act of serving a tennis ball. We cover each of them in some detail, piecing them together in the way we feel makes the most sense.

The first six are identified as preparatory measures. These are the steps the server should take in the course of getting the tools he will use properly positioned (racket in one hand, ball in the other), planning where the ball will be directed and how it will be struck, and taking the base line position and stance that will give him the best chance to realize that plan. They are, in order: Step One: The Grip (Racket); Step Two: The Hold (Ball); Step Three: The Decisions; Step Four: The Target; Step Five: The Position (Base Line); Step Six: The Stance.

The next five are identified as preliminary motions. These are the steps the server should consider taking immediately before the actual propelling actions are initiated. They involve a final body "tune-up," a last minute adjustment in how the ball to be served should be positioned for the lift, and the placement of the body and its extremities in its ultimate posture for the service delivery itself. They are, in order: Step Seven: The Respiration; Step Eight: The Lean; Step Nine: The Bounce (Ball); Step Ten: The Fingering (Ball); Step Eleven: The Recovery.

The last four are identified as propelling actions. These are the steps the server should take which, if properly coordinated, combine to make the actual service delivery actions—of head, body, arms, and legs—a single, smooth, well-timed operation. They are, in order: Step Twelve: The Lift (Ball); Step Thirteen: The Swing/

Strike/Swing; Step Fourteen: The Stride; Step Fifteen: The Finish.

While it is O.K. to view these fifteen steps as recognizably separate, they should never be considered as distinct or isolated entities complete unto themselves.

For purposes of teaching and learning, individual identification of the components in serving is, of course, necessary. But for purposes of practice and play, success as a server can only occur when the player has managed to meld these components into a well-balanced structure of mutually interdependent elements that gives the total service act a fluent rhythm from start to finish.

To kindle such an understanding, and to demonstrate how these fifteen steps fit together into a single harmonious pattern, the book contains some amount of repetition and considerable cross-reference. This built-in redundancy is particularly prevalent during the discussions of the four propelling actions—most of whose movements are complementally supporting to a marked degree. We feel this is the only way we can properly present the all-important simultaneity of many of these steps—and, in so doing, draw special attention to the fact that ultimately the several actions involved in the actual service delivery itself are really quite indivisible.

We have already stated in the Introduction that our book has been written for men *and* women.

Let us now proceed to clarify the dimensions of our audience a bit further by explaining that it has also been written for right-handers *and* left-handers.

Toward this latter end, we intend to follow the general practice of identifying various parts of the server's anatomy by using *ball* and *racket* as adjectives to designate the correct arm, leg, side of the body, etc., mentioned in the step being discussed. For example, when the server takes his stance, we specify that he places his ball foot forward—rather than clutter up the text with the extra words needed to explain that the right-handed server places his left foot forward, and the left-handed server places his right foot forward. As a consequence, the terms *left* and *right* will not, as a rule, be used for this purpose at all.

Some of the finest tennis players in the world swing from the port side. We hope our adapted terminology can help them keep on coming. The game would, indeed, be a far less interesting one without a Rod Laver, a Jimmy Connors, or a John McEnroe.

Whether you espouse all or only part of what we say about the serve is up to you.

We can guarantee it will give you something to think about.

And, as a minimum, it will furnish you with all kinds of raw material from which to construct your own modus operandi—if this, indeed, seems the preferable route for you to follow.

PART TWO

THE SERVE: PREPARATORY MEASURES

Step One: The Grip (Racket)
Step Two: The Hold (Ball)
Step Three: The Decisions
Step Four: The Target
Step Five: The Position (Base Line)
Step Six: The Stance

5 Step One: The Grip (Racket)

In any sport where a manually operated instrument is used to strike a ball, the novice can get off to a good start if he knows from the beginning how that instrument should be held in the hand.

At first, a prescribed grip may seem awkward and unnatural—as in golf and occasionally baseball. Fortunately, this does not often happen in tennis. When proper instruction is lacking at the outset, however, exceptions can occur. Take the case of the tyro who has yet to receive any directions but who has spent an appreciable amount of time playing *pat ball* or *badminton style* tennis—with the racket clutched in front of his face like a defensive shield. This sees him gripping the handle in the way he would pick up a racket lying flat on a table, and could develop a bad habit that might be difficult to break.

But enough of that.

Let's get on with the positive.

To grip a racket properly for the serve, a player should grasp the handle near its end while someone clasps the stringed surface of the frame between his palms in a vertical position and stands fronting the player in such a way that the handle can be pointed at the elbow of the player's racket arm as it hangs loosely at his side a foot or so away.

While his hand is still holding the racket, with the frame remaining in a plane perpendicular to the ground, the server should observe his grip carefully from above. If the racket has been grasped correctly:

1. the thumb and first finger have formed a "V" near the handle top's longitudinal edge that is on the same side as the thumb;
2. the three other fingers, all lightly touching each other, have circled three-quarters of the way around and under the handle;
3. the first finger has curled in the same direction up, halfway around and under the handle, with the tip joint resting against the handle's bottom side;
4. the thumb has curled in the opposite direction one-quarter of the way around the handle to a location between the tip of the first finger and the tip joint of the second finger;
5. the life line crease in the lower part of the hand is so positioned on the handle's top side that the grip is firmly supported by the two palm pads just above the wrist—the preponderance of that support being supplied by the pad connected with the last three fingers.

At the start of the swing the hold should be comfortable and compact—but not tight—with the pressure of palm, fingers, and thumb evenly distributed. While the fingers should be contracted around the handle just before striking the ball—to assure that the racket swings through the ball—care should be taken that the racket wrist remains supple at all times to permit maximum flexion and smooth timing.

Once the server has this grip down pat, he should stick with it. It is the best one to employ, since with little or no adjustment it can be used for all of the other tennis strokes except the forehand and forehand volley, which require the hand to shift so that the thumb and first finger form a "V" near the handle top's longitudinal edge that is on the same side as the first finger. Quite apart from any rationalization that teaching the serve deserves first priority attention, the very fact that the grip involved with shots played on the forehand side is unique is one of the best reasons for teaching the forehand *after* the serve. That it is customary to reverse the process is particularly hard to defend in those many cases when the instructor lets the pupil start off serving with the forehand grip because it is familiar, gradually shifting to the service grip over an extended period of time. From a practical point of view, it might very well be wiser to teach both the serve and backhand before the forehand, because the latter requires a different grip. But it is rarely done—more than likely because the instructor wants the beginner to sense the feeling of contacting ball with racket as soon as possible, and ground strokes on the forehand side seem the best way to accomplish this purpose.

Some servers insist on keeping the thumb relatively straight and bracing it against the thumb side of the handle in a position separated an inch or more from the other fingers. Others spread their fingers to cover more of the handle. While either variation—or a tandem of both—can give one a feeling of greater strength and control and can actually help a weak backhand stroke, these modifications definitely inhibit wrist action, the key to striking the serve with good speed and proper spin. If possible, the player should refrain from using either when making a service delivery.

A couple of additional suggestions.

First, don't be confused by dialogue insisting there are three basically sound tennis grips rather than two, i.e., that the best one for the serve places the hand halfway between the positions for the backhand and forehand. This is a refinement that is likely to be more worrisome than helpful.

Second, remember that the closer the service grip is to the one prescribed in this chapter, the nearer maximum the wrist bend can be during the swing and the wrist snap when the strike occurs. Actually the potential radius of wrist rotation for this service—or backhand—grip is significantly greater than for the forehand grip.

Finally, always keep the following in mind.

While there are a number of ways to serve, the adjustments involved in shifting from one type of delivery to another do not require a change in grip but, rather, a modification of one or more of the other fourteen steps in the service structure.

6 Step Two: The Hold (Ball)

The single most exacting step in the tennis serve is the lift of the ball, i.e., the movement that places the object to be struck in that airborne position where it can best be propelled by the racket into the opponent's court. Note that we do not use the word *toss* to describe this action, in recognition that the ball is not really propelled prior to the strike but merely lifted at a speed that allows it to leave the fingers and continue rising in the right direction to the proper height.

How the ball is positioned in the fingers for the lift will be covered in Chapter 14. How the ball is actually lifted will be covered in Chapter 16. For the moment, we will limit the discussion to the subject of what is held in the ball hand at the time these actions occur.

In the early years of the game it was customary for most tennis servers to hold two and occasionally three balls in the lifting hand prior to the beginning of a point. This was intended to be a timesaving act in anticipation that a large number of the points in a game require more than one serve to get a ball in play.

In relatively recent times, however, the fact that a good many players are turning to the use of two-handed strokes has seen a trend toward holding only one ball for each service. Further, many of our better players have come to see that holding more than one ball may be false economy as far as both accuracy and time are concerned. With a good serve relying on a good lift, and a good lift, for many, dependent, in large measure, on repeatedly holding a configuration of identical size, shape, and weight in the optimum manner, it seems questionable for the server to vary the number of balls he holds when service deliveries are made.

For one thing, since it can be easier to hold a single object in a consistently similar way than two and control the speed, direction, and height of its lift if a second object is not held in the same hand more than half the time, the margin of error can be minimized when a server holds only one ball, and more first serves are likely to go in as a result. Second, with a single ball, the server can more easily groove his lift/swing coordination so that eventually he is striking his first and second serves with the same rhythmic force—granted the second serve will normally have less speed and more spin to give it a better chance to land in play. More on this in Chapter 17. Finally, the fewer balls held in the hand during the lifting action, the easier it seems to be for many servers—most often those whose hands are not very big—to keep the rotation of the ball at a minimum when it rises into the air. Why this is important will be discussed in Chapter 14.

Some may argue that their first service delivery is different from their second, that the lift is not exactly the same for either, and that they can better execute the required lift for the first serve holding two balls and for the second serve holding one ball.

This may be all very well. But consider, for a moment, how much more flexible and effective his service game will be if a player can: (1) learn to lift one ball accurately in several ways for different serves; and, better yet, (2) learn to direct the ball so consistently well that he can successfully deliver a flat or spin service from the same kind of lift and make it less likely that his opponent can guess correctly what the next service delivery will be. We'll delve into this in more detail in Chapter 16.

While some of our finest players hold two balls for the first serve, it may be best, if you're just learning the game, to start off holding a single ball for each service delivery. If you do so, place a second ball in the ball side pocket of your tennis shorts before beginning a service point. A simple patch pocket attached to one side of a tennis skirt can accommodate the lady player. Should you be serving well, a large share of your first serves will be good, and you will be playing many points with a ball in your pocket. This suggests that you try keeping one there for all points whenever it is convenient for you to do so. It will not interfere with your game once your body and legs adjust to your carrying this small item of extra equipment.

If you've been playing the game for some time holding more than one ball for your first serve, try switching to one for a while. You may find that this will do more for the consistency, the accuracy, the pace, and the controlled flexibility of your service game than anything you have done for a long time.

Give it a fair shot.

There's a good chance you'll like it—particularly if your palms are small and your fingers short.

7 Step Three: The Decisions

That tennis is an episodic sport requiring the tennis player to make a decision every time he serves is often overlooked—or simply ignored—not only by many novices and a good number of instructors but frequently by the most experienced professionals.

To state it in slightly different terms, it is not just the beginner who can make the unforgivable error of stepping up and serving a ball willy-nilly. It is everyone who plays the game—particularly when fatigue starts to enervate the muscles and sap the concentration. This is true despite the recognition by most that a vital part of the serving process is thinking through in advance what to try—and then actually trying it—being prepared, of course, to accept the disappointment that willing the act may not bring it off in a large number of cases.

Planning the delivery of the serve—and registering in the mind's eye an image of what is intended—should occur in the serving delivery sequence as soon as the server has his racket in one hand and a ball in the other. It should never be delayed until the actual service action is under way. Lack of decision, or agonizing about an unsure decision, during the beginning of the swing/strike/swing can get the server thinking too hard and doing too little—with catastrophic results.

There are several decisions to be made. Because they are interdependent, they should be considered by the server in the following order.

First, he should decide where to aim his serve, i.e., what his target will be (see Chapter 8).

Next, he should decide where to stand, i.e., what position behind the base line he will take to aim at his target (see Chapter 9).

Finally, he should decide how to stand. In doing so, he should keep in mind that the stance selected may determine the most advantageous direction for the ball to be lifted—and that the lift made will determine how the racket should be swung and the ball most productively struck, as well as the most accommodating stride and finish that can follow.

As pointed out in the first chapter, the server can choose from a number of alternatives in deciding where and how to direct the ball. The selection he finally makes depends on such variables as the relative strengths and weaknesses in the overall ability, mental attitude, and physical endurance of the player and his opponent, the closeness of the score, the angle of the sun's rays, the general visibility in the playing area, the direction and velocity of the wind, the composition and general condition of the court's surface, and the relative condition of the tennis balls in play.

Once the server recognizes the importance of evaluating and determining how to counter these variables, he finds that the time to do so requires only a few seconds. But it must be done. And subjectively—not by happenstance. If making these decisions is disregarded, the effectiveness of the most important element in tennis—the serve—is badly handicapped.

When the reader has covered all of the fifteen steps in the service act as described in this book, he should return to this chapter and think through, in their proper order, the decisions that should be made at this point in the serving process. It is likely to mean more to him then than it does now.

One final word.

When you are serving, give full credence to the advantage you have over your opponent in the fact that by showing serving the attention it deserves you can do much to control approximately half of the match in much the same way that a pitcher does in baseball or a quarterback in football.

Don't throw away this advantage by neglect.

It can cost you if you ever want to be a good tennis player.

8 Step Four: The Target

In Chapter 7 we pointed out that the first decision the server must make is determine where his serve will be aimed.

Since his objective is to direct the ball on successive points into one of the two service courts, the server has two problems (see Figure 1): (1) determine what his target will be in the right service court 1X; (2) determine what his target will be in the left service court 2X.

The selection of a target depends in large measure on two considerations, which, unfortunately, are not necessarily complementary. One poses the question "Should the server aim at a target from which it will be difficult for the receiver to make an effective return?" The other poses the question "Should the server aim at a target which, if missed, is more likely to keep the ball in play?"

While these considerations become less important the more a server improves his delivery, it makes sense for the unfinished player, with two opportunities to get the ball in play for each tennis point, to gravitate toward: (1) "making it more difficult for the receiver to return" when selecting the target for his first serve; and (2) "making it easier for the server to keep the ball in play" when selecting the target for his second serve.

Let's look at each of these premises in more detail.

SERVICE TARGETS

⊙ Targets most often causing right-handed (RH) or left-handed (LH) receiver maximum difficulty if server is right-handed—with side line targets reversed if server is left-handed

RECEIVER

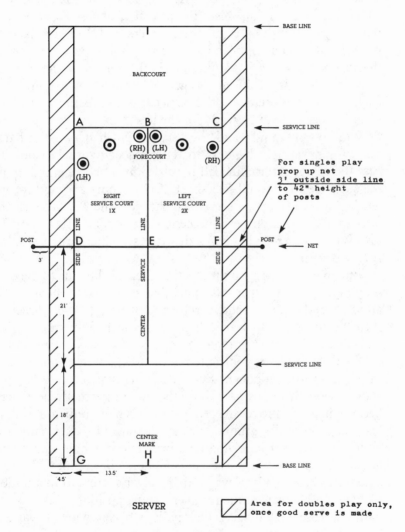

SERVER

⊙ Targets affording server maximum margin of error

FIGURE 1

More Difficult to Return. The great majority of tennis players have stronger forehands than backhands. And all players have more difficulty accurately and effectively returning a deep serve than a shallow one because: (1) the size of the angle within which the receiver can select the direction of his return is less—thereby inhibiting that return's effectiveness; (2) the receiver does not have as good an opportunity to return the serve by taking it on the rise and putting it away; and (3) the return of the ball must travel further, is in the air longer, is slowed down more by air friction as a result, lands with less pace, and gives the server a split second more time to be ready for the next shot.

With this in mind—and the server right-handed—the hardest serve for most right-handers to return (see Figure 1) lands deep near the center service line EB toward B in court 1X and deep near the side line FC several feet short of C in court 2X; and for most left-handers to return, a serve near the side line DA but well short of A in 1X and deep near the center service line EB toward B in 2X. With the server left-handed, these side line targets would be reversed.

Some receivers insist on protecting their backhands to the extent of gambling with return positions that may enable them to "step around" and make forehand returns off many serves directed at their backhands. This leaves them dangerously vulnerable to deliveries directed at their extreme forehands.

When the server is confronted with either of these situations, he can cross up his opponent by shifting his first serve to targets in court 1X or 2X opposite to those that might normally be expected because it allows the receiver to make a forehand return, most often his most powerful ground stroke weapon. In exercising these options, the player is relying on a principle in tennis tactics which tends to be ignored: that a server can often win a point with relative ease if he occasionally plays to the receiver's strength in a trade-off that takes advantage of the receiver's court position weakness.

In the case of the serve that pulls a player wide, toward and beyond either of the doubles alleys, the receiver is often forced to make a return down the nearest sideline—a maneuver that is not always easy to perform. This, at least, can introduce an additional element of difficulty for these two targets in the event that the receiver's backhand is stronger than his forehand—a circumstance that is not as unusual as many people think. And in the case of the finished player, who possesses good ground strokes, both to port and starboard, these are the targets that actually produce a large number of aces in expert competition.

There is one target selection that does not get the recognition it merits: the serve aimed to bounce toward the receiver's navel, via either a hard flat delivery or a lively spin delivery, that moves the ball in from the forehand or backhand side. Such a stratagem can be particularly effective against a player whose reflexes are a little slow, making it difficult for him to decide in time whether he should move right or left to get in position to make a good shot. When this occurs, one or more of the following can take place: the receiver is caught off balance, swings off the wrong foot, or executes a stroke that is badly constricted because it is made too close to the body. In such circumstances his return often goes out of court or sets up an easy winner for the server.

Easier to Keep in Play. A player may be inclined to feel that it's best to direct his second serves toward a location in his opponent's court where he has managed to get the highest percentage of his first serves. But, if he really wants to consider a target which, if missed, is more likely to keep the ball in play because it affords the maximum margin of error, he will aim at an area that is: roughly halfway between the center service line and side line (see Figure 1); and within some two to four feet of the receiver's service line—where most second serves will go no matter what the server's intent. As he becomes more proficient as a server, this safety factor need no longer be so stringent, and the player can enlarge his target area accordingly.

This brings us to a discussion of the double fault and the fact—which may surprise a lot of people—that its curse can be somewhat overemphasized by many who teach and play the game with some authority.

Actually there are three kinds of double faults: (1) the serve into the net; (2) the serve wide of the service court; (3) the serve beyond the service line.

The second serve into the net is pretty hard to defend because it usually is caused by careless service mechanics—most often a lift that is too low or badly directed. And there is little excuse for the second serve that lands to the right or left of the receiver's service court—beyond the stress factor it may set up in the receiver's subconscious that is similar to the feelings of a batter facing a pitcher whose throws are hard to anticipate because they can occasionally be wild. But the second serve that lands between the receiver's center service line and side line but beyond the receiver's service line is another story and does not necessarily deserve the censure it receives, as long as its frequency does not get out of hand.

Given a few moments' thought, the reason should be obvious: it's rather difficult on the one hand to justify that the second serve must have depth to be considered a good one—as in the case of a ground stroke—and on the other hand to be far more critical if a service delivery lands beyond the service line than if a forehand or backhand drive goes beyond the base line. The key questions are: (1) How many second serves in a match probably won points because they were deep that would, just as probably, have lost points had they been short? (2) How many second serves were double faults because they landed between the receiver's center service line and side line but beyond the receiver's service line? If he feels that his total in (1) can be greater than his total in (2), the server stands to benefit no matter what the total in (2) happens to be—and he gets an extra "A" for effort. In any event, the fact still remains—to quote the old saw—"when neither the first nor second serve goes in, it's nobody's fault but your own."

There are a number of factors that exercise a lot of leverage on the likelihood that a player can successfully hit a service target. Some of the most important are: the position behind the base line from which the serve is delivered; the proximity of the target; the size of the target; the depth the serve may go and still end up in play; and the height of the net over which the serve is directed. All of these items will be discussed in Chapter 9. Later on still, in Chapters 10, 16, and 17, we shall see that the success or failure of the serve may be dependent on such additional service restrictions as the stance assumed, the lift made, and the stroke selected for the strike. And in Chapter 21 we shall learn that the environment and the character of the court, racket, and balls used during play can limit a player's service options.

As these various constraints are altered, the targets become either easier or harder to realize. This is particularly true when the server opts for the more extreme—and, therefore, less attainable—targets, where success can normally be expected only if these several constraints are associated in the most favorable mix with each other.

In the course of a tennis match, it is not unusual to find that the first serves of many of our finest tennis players not only miss their targets but fail to put the ball in play as much as 50 percent of the time, or more. A good deal of this poor performance can relate to the fact that on a number of occasions even the experts do not properly pick out and concentrate on a target for this most important of the game's attacking weapons. On the other hand, of course, part of this failure can also relate to their attempting to home in on targets that are too refined to be realistic.

The server's knowledge and expectancy that he may miss a target a good share of the time is neither an excuse for not having a target nor a justification for not making a real effort to hit it.

The extra attention is worth it.

Don't ever think it isn't.

9 Step Five: The Position (Base Line)

In Chapter 7 we pointed out that once the target has been selected at which the serve will be aimed, the server must next determine where he should stand to make the service delivery.

Since his objective is to direct the ball on successive points into one of the two service courts, the server has two problems: (1) determine his position to the right of his court's base line center mark H and behind his right base line when serving the ball into the right service court 1X (see Figure 2); (2) determine his position to the left of his court's base line center mark H and behind his left base line when serving the ball into the left service court 2X.

Key factors to be considered are:

1. the nearer the server's starting position is to a location from which he may have to travel the least laterally in any one direction to reach the receiver's return, the greater chance he has to win the point;

2. the nearer the server's starting position is to the optimum forecourt position for a winning volley of the receiver's return (normally some ten to twenty feet from the net in a position that is roughly beneath the line of flight taken by the served ball), the greater

HOW RIGHT-HANDED SERVER'S POSITION
CAN EFFECT
RECEIVER'S POSITION

Slightly curved lines drawn from H and J bracket outer limits of directions served ball may go and realistically expect to land in play

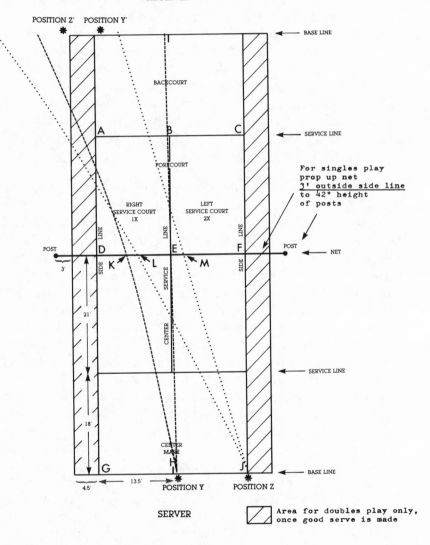

RECEIVER

For singles play
prop up net
3' outside side line
to 42" height
of posts

SERVER

Area for doubles play only,
once good serve is made

FIGURE 2

the server's chances of making such a shot successfully. Further on this in Chapter 19;

3. the nearer the server's starting position is to the
target area in the receiver's court, the greater the
velocity of the served ball's impact in that area and
the more effective the bounce resulting from any
spin imparted by the service delivery;

4. the nearer the server's starting position is to the
point from which a delivery can be most easily made
to the midpoint of the receiver's service line (point B
in Figure 2—the one where the average server scores
most of his aces), the greater the server's chances of
hitting that target with what is normally a fast serve
that is flat or slightly sliced.

Even the most casual study of Figure 2 shows that the closer the
player serves from a position just to the right or left of H (or,
conversely, the farther he stands to the left of J—or right of G) the
better off he will be on the first three of the above counts. To be
specific: (1) the maximum distance the server must travel laterally
in any one direction from H is 13½ feet less than from J, or G; (2)
the optimum forecourt position for a winning volley averages some
two feet closer from H than from J, or G; (3) the receiver's service
line averages some 3 feet closer from H than from J, or G.

What may not be entirely obvious is why the server's chances of
hitting point B in Figure 2 are better the nearer the server's starting
position is to H. Actually there are three reasons.

The first has very little real significance: that at H the server is
1½ feet—or about 2½ percent—closer to B than at either J or G.

The second is somewhat more meaningful: that the height of the
net over which the served ball must pass to hit point B from point J
or G is almost 1¾ inches—or about 5 percent—higher than the
height of the net at point E, over which the served ball must pass to
hit point B from H. This assumes, of course, that the net has been
properly hung, i.e., at a height of 36 inches at the exact center of the
court and 42 inches—or 16.67 percent higher—at the two positions,
three feet outside each of the singles court's side lines, where the net

for a doubles court should be propped up to post heights for singles play.

It is the third reason that is really important: that the server's allowable depth margin of error is minimum at J or G and maximum at H if he is trying to hit B. This means that if he aims from J or G and hits short of B, via lines drawn from J or G to B, his ball is most likely to land in the wrong service court. It also means that if he aims from H and hits short of B, via a line drawn from H to B, his shot has a good chance of nipping the center service line BE and be in play.

Some justifiable modifications in position are made for reasons which may or may not be directly related to the serve itself. For example, it is helpful for the right-handed server to stand three or four feet to the left of H when addressing the right-handed receiver in the left service court 2X. This not only enhances the chances of making a good serve to the receiver's backhand but also gives some protection to the server's own backhand—if it is weak—by narrowing the width of the target area at which the receiver must aim to make a return to that side. Similar adjustments to the right or left of H can be made to accommodate other combinations of right-handed or left-handed servers and receivers. Basically, however, serving will benefit most from a position near H.

There are other less important considerations which would say that an occasional serve from a position closer to J or G can be a useful ploy. These are worthy of some attention—particularly for the more finished player who already possesses a better than average service delivery.

For one thing, the nearer a server stands to these extreme right or left positions on the base line, the wider the receiver must stand to return the serve—a situation which may confuse him by changing the angle of his return. Figure 2 demonstrates this by showing: (1) that when a right-handed server stands in position Y to serve into the right service court 1X, the receiver should stand in the vicinity of position Y'; (2) when this same server stands in position Z to serve into the same court, the receiver should stand in the vicinity of position Z'—several feet outside and behind his court. These positions permit the receiver to cope with a possible slice that bounces away from him and forces him to move to his right—positions that may end up even farther to his right if the court surface is faster. This same problem with the slice exists if the left service court 2X if the server is left-handed but disappears when the right-hander serves into the left service court 2X or the left-hander serves into the right service court 1X.

For another thing, the nearer a server stands to these extreme right or left positions on the base line, the greater the depth of the deepest potential target and the easier it is for the server—particularly if he is not very tall—to deliver a hard serve with a flat trajectory that will end up in play. This is again illustrated in Figure 2. The deepest potential target from J (point A) is almost 7 percent greater in depth than the deepest potential target from H (again point A). The same comparison exists between G and H with relation to point C.

For still another thing, the nearer a server stands to these extreme right or left positions on the base line, the lower the mean height of the net over which he must serve to hit within the limitations of a realistically attainable target area in his opponent's service court (see Figures 2 and 3). In point of fact, the average net height differential above 36 inches which fronts this kind of target area from H (as represented by the line KE) is approximately 50 percent more than that fronting a similar kind of target area from J (as represented by the line LM). This comparison between H and J is exactly the same as a similar comparison between H and G. While this differential is measured in inches—with the maximum being 3½ inches at K as shown in Figure 3—the effect on the service can be more significant than one might suppose.

Following such a base line position strategy for a serve every now and then might be helpful—and often with diametrically different objectives in mind.

For example, if a server is at forty love or forty fifteen on his own serve, a first service from a position closer to J or G can occasionally produce an ace when the server aims at either the right or left side of his realistic target area. If the target is missed, little may be lost. On the other hand, if the target is hit, the effect on the opponent can be very demoralizing.

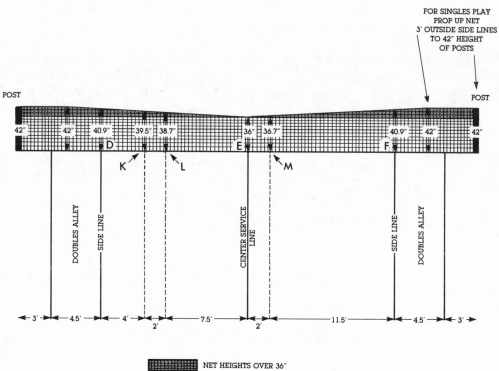

NET HEIGHTS
FOR
SINGLES PLAY

FOR SINGLES PLAY
PROP UP NET
3' OUTSIDE SIDE LINES
TO 42" HEIGHT
OF POSTS

POST

POST

42" 42" 40.9" 39.5" 38.7" 36" 36.7" 40.9" 42" 42"

D
K
L
E
M
F

DOUBLES ALLEY

SIDE LINE

CENTER SERVICE
LINE

SIDE LINE

DOUBLES ALLEY

3' 4.5' 4' 2' 7.5' 2' 11.5' 4.5' 3'

NET HEIGHTS OVER 36"

FIGURE 3

In other circumstances, if the receiver is properly timing the server's delivery with consistent regularity and winning a number of points with good service returns, a change of direction brought about by serving occasionally from a position closer to J or G can often give the receiver something else to think and, perhaps, worry about.

Whatever the case, wherever you do decide to stand, be sure you do not commit a foot fault by touching the base line with either foot before you strike the ball with your serve. Form the habit of standing several inches behind that line when you take your stance, and this is unlikely to occur.

To repeat what we have already said: the odds against service errors in tandem with the odds in favor of service winners make a very strong case for you to serve from a point near your center mark.

But once your delivery is a reasonably sound stroke, you may want to shift your position around every now and then.

It can keep your opponent off balance, harass his concentration, confuse his defensive pattern and start him guessing—all perfectly legitimate maneuvers and frequently productive ways to change the momentum of a match or complete an opponent's collapse.

10 Step Six: The Stance

In Chapter 7 we pointed out that once the server has determined where he should stand to aim at the target selected, he must next decide how he should stand to make the service delivery. This means, for the most part, how to angle his feet behind the base line.

We also pointed out in Chapter 7 that the stance selected may determine the most advantageous direction for the ball to be lifted—and that the lift made will determine how the racket should be swung and the ball most productively struck, as well as the most accommodating stride and finish that can follow. This interrelationship can make the stance decision a multipurpose one that requires, in addition, the concomitant resolution of such collateral questions as "What kind of service stroke shall I use (slice, flat, top spin, or American twist)?" and "Will I advance to the net immediately after serving the ball?" We'll develop these associations further in Chapters 16, 17, 18, and 19.

It is not our intention, however, to imply that there is a single optimum way for the feet to be angled in serving that best reconciles these several considerations.

Quite the contrary.

The server actually has a good many ways he can position his feet as long as he stands behind the base line; directs his head toward the service court target; stations his body in an upright posture that is facing toward and roughly parallel to the intended flight of the serve; and keeps the following additional limitations in mind:

1. the distance between the big toes should be approximately the width of the server's shoulders;
2. a straight line from the big toe of the back foot through the big toe of the front foot should point at or slightly toward the ball arm side of the midpoint of the potential target area in the court toward which the serve will be directed.

Figure 4 illustrates the position of the feet used most widely by a right-handed server when aiming serves from a point just to the right of the server's center mark to a target area about halfway between the center service line and side line in the right service court. There are, of course, a number of other perfectly satisfactory stances. In addition, there are an infinite number of directions in which the player can serve from an infinite number of positions behind the base line. The principal thing to remember is that a change in the intended direction of the serve and/or the selected position on the base line may require an adjustment in the stance.

It should also be noted that there are bona fide reasons why some stances are impractical—even though they meet the two limitations described above. For example, positioning the two feet in a "tight-rope" position when the body itself is facing toward the intended flight of the serve would unnaturally contort the torso and threaten the server's stance stability. Further, any stance that sees one or both feet in a turned-in, "pigeon-toed" position would also impair the equilibrium as well as handicap any advance to the net the server may wish to make after the delivery—a subject we will cover in Chapter 19.

What is needed at all times is balance—no matter what the combination of foot angles be.

This can best be supplied by limiting the forward direction of either foot to positions pointing at angles between forty-five and ninety degrees to the intended flight of the serve. In truth, most players will find it preferable, most of the time, to maintain the perpendicular (or ninety degree) position of the back foot with relation to the intended flight of the serve for all deliveries, limiting any real change to the front foot only (see Figure 4). If nothing more, this will permit the server to brace the back foot more firmly on the ground at the termination of the recovery (see Chapter 15).

We will describe the most useful stances in Chapter 16 in the course of explaining how the stance may affect the server's lift, and how the lift links the stance with the swing/strike/swing, the stride, and the finish. Suffice it to say at this juncture that: (1) the more the front foot is positioned perpendicular to the intended flight of the serve the easier it can be for the server to strike an American twist when delivery is made; and (2) the more the front foot is aimed at approximately a forty-five degree angle with the intended flight of the serve the easier it is to strike any serve but the American twist when delivery is made. These points notwithstanding, it usually makes most sense for the novice to select that single combination of recommended foot angles for his stance that seems most comfortable, and maintain it until his game has advanced beyond the beginning stages. In actual fact, it is the average player, particularly when he becomes older and less agile, who may be able to benefit most by modifying his stance for different types of service deliveries. At the more proficient end of the playing spectrum the need to use different relative foot positions becomes less important, with the finished professional sticking basically to a single stance posture for all lifts, strikes, and finishes—much like a good batter in baseball often insists on using his own "template," if you will, when he literally "digs in" at the plate in the way he likes best every time he comes up to hit.

In determining his stance, the server is confronted once again with the dual problems of directing the ball on successive points into one of the two service courts. Since the angles at which the server's feet should be positioned with respect to the base line in the left service court are quite different from the angles with the base line in the right service court, we have included a Figure 5, illustrating the position of the feet used most widely by a right-

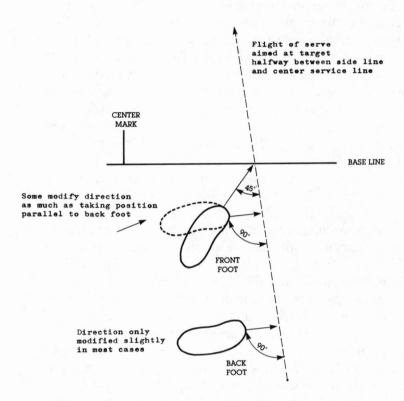

Flight of serve
aimed at target
halfway between side line
and center service line

CENTER
MARK

BASE LINE

Some modify direction
as much as taking position
parallel to back foot

45°

90°

FRONT
FOOT

Direction only
modified slightly
in most cases

90°

BACK
FOOT

In above positions line between big toes approximates width of shoulders
and parallels flight of serve

FIGURE 4

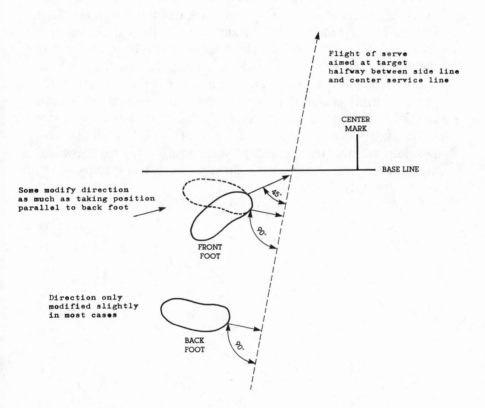

RIGHT-HANDER'S FOOT POSITIONS
MOST WIDELY USED
WHEN SERVICE INTO
LEFT SERVICE COURT

Flight of serve
aimed at target
halfway between side line
and center service line

CENTER
MARK

BASE LINE

Some modify direction
as much as taking position
parallel to back foot

45°

90°

FRONT
FOOT

Direction only
modified slightly
in most cases

BACK
FOOT

90°

In above positions line between big toes approximates width of shoulders
and parallels flight of serve

FIGURE 5

handed server when aiming serves from a point just to the left of the server's center mark to a target area about halfway between the center service line and side line in the left service court.

The fact that the right side of the court is a "flip-over" facsimile of the left makes it possible to get a quick fix on the position of the feet used most widely by left-handed servers. By holding a mirror on edge in a vertical position alongside and an inch to the right of the illustrated portion of, first, Figure 4 and, second, Figure 5, so that it reflects the part to be studied, it can be readily seen from the "reverse print" images thus generated that the foot positions shown for the right-handed player serving into, first, the right service court and, second, the left service court will furnish the foot positions for the left-handed player serving into, first, the left service court and, second, the right service court, respectively.

Southpaws take note.

Once again we haven't forgotten you're there.

PART THREE

THE SERVE: PRELIMINARY MOTIONS

Step Seven: The Respiration
Step Eight: The Lean
Step Nine: The Bounce (Ball)
Step Ten: The Fingering (Ball)
Step Eleven: The Recovery

11 Step Seven: The Respiration

Generally speaking, our anatomy of the tennis serve embraces two kinds of preliminary, "get set" motions.

In one category are the contrived physical motions which the server meaningfully initiates to generate body strength and sharpen mental perception. In a second category are the spontaneous nervous motions which the server involuntarily adopts to relieve body tension and promote mental relaxation.

Both kinds are important.

But only the contrived motions can be recommended on the basis of any sort of scientific rationale or endorsed by way of actual experience. The spontaneous motions are, for the most part, concocted by each individual to meet what he feels are his own needs. They can—and do—cover a wide range of unwitting fidgets that do not lend themselves to any real analysis. We only mention them in passing.

Given the few seconds afforded the server for the preliminary motions, in toto, there is little time for him to crank up any planned movements that are either intricate or sophisticated.

Actually he has time for only five very simple ones.

The first is concerned with the way the server performs the act of respiration, i.e., the inhalation and exhalation of air during the delivery sequence. Since it is not really a mandatory ingredient of the service structure, however, an established breathing pattern should be considered optional only. But it does have a tangible purpose that can contribute appreciably to service success: to give the blood flowing in the circulatory system a heavy dose of oxygen, which will tone up the muscles, alert the brain, and prepare both for the exertion to follow. And it can be helpful to many players—particularly those who tighten up and/or tire easily.

Only in the last several decades has deep breathing received the measure of recognition its benefit to sports deserves. Prior to World War II its role in the preliminary motions of any significant athletic exertion was primarily an instinctive one in those relatively few cases where its value was utilized to any marked degree. Track competitors—particularly high jumpers and broad jumpers—would oxygenate with some frequency to counter stress and maintain composure but rarely made it a must in the regimen demanded by good technique.

One of the first times it was used as a planned stratagem—presumably with its true merit in mind—was in basketball by the professional star St. Louis Hawk Bob Pettit in connection with foul shooting, an art at which he was an established expert. Others followed Bob's lead, and today a large number of both amateur and professional hoopsters use the technique he first made popular: to fill the lungs with air just before addressing one's self to the task of trying to toss the ball through the basket from the free-throw line.

Respiration is presently a commonly used device in such sports as golf, bowling, and swimming. That a good many of its proponents still conceive of it as chiefly a reliever and relaxer—rather than a strengthener and sharpener—is not all that important. The principal thing is to give the respiratory motion a precise function in the overall structure of the athletic action of which it is, literally, such a vital part—rather than allow it to remain a sometime maneuver that may only be employed subconsciously from time to time, particularly when fatigue has the body all but crying out for more air.

In tennis the server starts his contrived respiration immediately after he has assumed his stance, with ball and racket at waist level. There are two deep breath inhalations and exhalations that take place back to back and bracket, in order: (1) the other preliminary motions and (2) the subsequent propelling actions.

In the first one the stance position is held while air is inhaled through the mouth. When lungs are full, the carbon dioxide is retained for a split second and then exhaled slowly, again through the mouth. This expiration actually parallels the lean, the bounce of the ball, the positioning of the fingers around the ball, the recovery, and the final set posture that is taken just prior to initiating the propelling actions—which follow almost immediately.

In the second one—after a pause during which the lungs are momentarily empty—the air should again be inhaled through the mouth until the lungs are full, in parallel with the downward and upward arm movement of the lift and the first part of the swing/ strike/swing; retained for a split second as the ball leaves the lifting hand and the racket is cocked behind the back; and then exhaled quickly and forcibly at exactly the same time the strike is made. We'll touch on this again in Chapters 16 and 17.

Once the timing of the server's breathing has been synchronized with those steps, which are simultaneous, proper respiration becomes second nature.

There is nothing difficult about it at all.

And when a player has it down pat, it will not only be of great therapeutic value but help bracket the time frame for any cadence he may desire to formulate in his mind to establish a good rhythm for these several movements—particularly the propelling actions that are involved in actually delivering the serve across the net. More on this in Chapter 16.

The foregoing rationale notwithstanding, dimensioning the tempo of the breathing done in conjunction with a tennis serve is not a must and should never be permitted to interfere with simultaneous preliminary motions or propelling actions in the serving process. If it appears to do so, forget it. Should a player find it preferable to let this respiration be spontaneous, so be it.

But it can be helpful to a beginner for the reasons described above. And even a more finished player who does not make a general practice of employing a contrived respiration approach can benefit if he recognizes its values and knows how to use it at the end of a long match when he is on the brink of bogging down physically and mentally.

12 Step Eight: The Lean

Immediately after completing the first inhalation, the server begins the second preliminary motion—the lean.

This sees him simultaneously performing the following diverse but integrated acts: starting the first contrived exhalation (see Chapter 11), he shifts his weight to the front foot, with front knee slightly bent, leans forward, and bounces the ball to be served (see Chapter 13). The lean is held through the subsequent catching and fingering of the ball (see Chapter 14), as a backward sweep of the racket gives the body a final impetus downward that actually raises the rear heel off the ground. The lean is concluded with the start of the recovery (see Chapter 15).

There are three reasons for the lean.

The first and most important one is that it increases the surge of blood circulation from heart to brain that originated with the first contrived inhalation by bending the head forward and neutralizing much of the gravitational force that makes it more difficult for the blood to flow upward from the cardiac pump to the cranium.

The second is that it facilitates placing the hand, holding the ball, in the proper position to execute the trial bounce and recapture of the ball, and final positioning of the fingers around the ball—subjects that will be covered in Chapters 13 and 14.

The third is that it establishes the proper plane of body action for the recovery—a subject that will be covered in Chapter 15. Actually the two motions are in exactly opposite directions—the lean toward the bounce, and the recovery away from the bounce.

One word of caution for some of you who may be too eager.

Don't exaggerate the motion of the lean by bending too far forward from the stand-up position.

The movement should never be unduly enervating but, rather, a slowly paced, almost deliberate cranking up of the service delivery that is soon to follow.

13 Step Nine: The Bounce (Ball)

There is some justification for questioning whether there is a real need to bounce the ball to be served just prior to the start of the server's propelling actions.

The reason could be that it may seem difficult to classify the bounce as a legitimate preliminary motion. Certainly if the action is really nothing more than the spontaneous nervous movement of the more restless players, it does not deserve to be included as a major component in the structure of the tennis serve.

But the bounce does make some real contributions to the service act, and, despite an apparently moot categorical authenticity, our designation of the bounce as Step Nine would imply that we feel it qualifies as a preliminary motion in its own right. We do—in light of the following considerations.

First of all, the bounce not only directly supplements the lean by holding the body in a bent-forward position for an extra second or so of accelerated blood flow to the brain but it gives the server an "excuse" for the lean—a bowing motion that, without an end purpose, would not only appear awkward and unnecessary to those watching who do not recognize its therapeutic value, but also would rarely be performed by the server solely on its own merit.

Second, whether contrived or spontaneous, the bounce does relieve tension while affording the server an additional second or two to review how he intends to strike the ball.

Third, the bounce permits the server to judge the texture and resilience of the ball he is about to serve. This can be more important in an informal competition where the balls can eventually appear to differ because they are likely to be used for several sets—less important in a major tournament where new balls will come into play several times in the same match. In a sense the bounce is a practice movement that gives the server a feel for one of the tools to be used in the ensuing play. This makes it comparable, in a somewhat farfetched sense, to the practice swing of a golf club before the actual shot. After all, when one stops to think about it, making a dry run swing with the racket at thin air—a possible "tool checking" alternative—would be pretty tiring and could even telegraph the kind of delivery the server intends to strike.

Fourth, the bounce gives the server the opportunity to move the ball from a loose hold in the hand to a correct position in the fingers (see Chapter 14) in preparation for the lift.

And fifth, the bounce signals the receiver that the server is prepared to start the play and makes it unlikely that there will be a "quick serve," i.e., one that does not give the receiver adequate time to prepare for his return. This is a courtesy that is appreciated by many and doesn't cost the server a thing.

With the above in mind, bounce the ball a foot or so ahead of the front toes, releasing it approximately at knee level about the time the racket arm begins a backward sweep of the racket to complete the lean (see Chapter 12), and catching it about the time the racket arm begins a forward sweep of the racket to start the recovery (see Chapter 15). While it is only necessary to do it once, there is nothing wrong with bouncing the ball several times if this seems more natural—as long as extending the movement does not seriously interfere with the timing of parallel preliminary motions.

14 Step Ten: The Fingering (Ball)

We have identified how the server positions his fingers around the tennis ball as a preliminary motion primarily because it takes place chronologically after the start of the first exhalation, the finish of the lean, and the completion of the bounce. Were this not the case, it might be more meaningful to classify this step as the last of the preparatory measures. Whether it is called one or the other has little real import, however, as long as the server is aware of how instrumental these finger positions are in successfully realizing what we have already identified several times as the most exacting step in the tennis serve—the lift of the ball.

As soon as the server catches the ball as it rises from the bounce, he should position it between the top joints of the thumb, first finger, and second finger—with the third and little fingers folded in slightly toward the palm if no second ball is also being held.

By simply "cradling" the ball in this fashion the server actually precludes the need to release the ball in any way during the lift, i.e., it literally takes off by itself as it rises beyond the server's reach. This means, of course, that the fingertips must gently support the ball to be served without actually grasping it—our reason for using the term *fingering* rather than one that denotes gripping or clutching.

If the ball is held in any other way, i.e., in the palm, or between the tips of the thumb and first finger (requiring tightening the hold to keep it steady), or cupped with three or four fingers surrounding it, the server must open or has a tendency to open the fingers to some extent when the lifted ball leaves the hand. Since the timing of this release action can deviate measurably under such conditions, an added variable is introduced that makes it more difficult to groove the height and direction of the lift, and give it the consistency it deserves.

In Chapter 6 it was pointed out that there are several reasons why there is a trend that sees a good many players holding only a single ball for each service, one being that the fewer balls held in the hand during the lifting action, the easier it seems to be, in most cases, for servers with small hands to keep the rotation of the ball at a minimum when it rises into the air.

Some may be wondering, "Why the big deal about lifting the ball with minimum spin?"

It's a good question for which we feel we have an equally good answer: the fewer revolutions the ball experiences while rising during the lift, the easier it is for the server to direct the ball to a location in the air where he desires to strike it. This will be explored in more detail in Chapters 16 and 17.

To repeat: at the end of the bounce, position the ball between the top joints of the thumb and first two fingers in a three-pronged prop of digit tips.

And as the forward sweep of the racket begins (see Chapter 15) let the body start the rise to an upright posture in connection with the recovery which immediately follows.

15 Step Eleven: The Recovery

Up to now we've stuck to tennis expressions which are probably familiar—at least in some measure—to a good number of our readers.

It is, therefore, with some qualms that we toss in a term of our own making—the *recovery*.

Fundamentally, the recovery is the motion in which the body straightens rather deliberately to an upright posture at the conclusion of the lean. The chief force generating the recovery is the forward sweep of the racket that starts as soon as the ball is caught after the bounce. This sweep continues upward until the racket top is about at eye level over the front knee. Simultaneously, the ball hand is raised to approximately shoulder level at a location adjacent to—but not touching—the racket, with the ball palm turned toward the server's face; the body weight is shifted from the front to back foot, while both knees remain relatively straight; the heel of the front foot is hoisted an inch or so, as the back foot is braced firmly on the ground; and the first contrived exhalation is concluded—with the breath held for an extra second or two while the final stand-up recovery position remains stationary.

There are a few things about the recovery that warrant special attention.

First, while the ball remains cupped in the fingers, you may find it helpful if you don't touch it to the racket at any time during the recovery motion—or afterward. This can tighten the fingering of the ball during the ensuing lift—making the results erratic and inaccurate—and disrupt the smoothness and timing of the downward action of the pre-strike swing described in Chapter 17.

Second, in preparation for the exertion to follow, optimize striking the serve with uniform power by purposefully relaxing the arms and upper torso during the breath-holding pause at the end of the recovery that precedes the second contrived inhalation. This relieves the muscles used in the propelling actions from the additional burden of vying with any rigidity in other muscles that can generate contrary or counteractive action.

Third, concentrate on bracing the back foot firmly on the ground to steady the raised heel of the front foot. This will better control the desired direction of the lift when it is finally made; help the server get up on his toes and start his stride across the base line; and supply some extra momentum to the swing/strike/swing, the stride, and the finish. John Newcombe is particularly adept at using the rear foot as an effective launching pad for advancing to the net after the service delivery.

Some further rationalization may help explain our predilection for pinpointing the recovery as one of our fifteen steps in the structure of the serve.

Bear with us while we give it a try.

Although our basic analysis of the serve's component parts in Chapter 4 placed special emphasis on the desirability of a fluent rhythm in the total service act, it should be noted at this point that the tennis serve does involve two recognizable breaks in movement continuity.

Both are normally momentary.

The first takes place after the stance has been set at the end of the preparatory measures—just before the first contrived inhalation, immediately preceding the beginning of the preliminary motions. The second takes place with the completion of the recovery at the end of the preliminary motions—just after the first contrived exhalation has been finished, and the breath is being held briefly prior to the start of the second contrived inhalation and the beginning of the propelling actions. In other words, these two break points are bench marks that actually bracket the beginning and end of the first contrived respiration.

The first break is not too consequential, since it occurs before the tempo of the service act is really initiated. While it normally involves no more than a few seconds, it can take longer without causing any mishap in the service pattern.

But the second break is significant for a very good reason: it affords the server a final respite just before the strenuous propelling actions begin. This permits him to prepare not only physically but mentally for the coordination and concentration required to make the actual service delivery a success.

In concluding the preliminary motions, the average server is likely to find that it is best for both racket frame and ball hand to end up no lower than shoulder level. Whatever the case, the ball hand should not be allowed to drop down with the ball to crotch level at the end of the recovery if the racket hand continues to hold the frame at a higher level. When this occurs, not only is the downward movement of the lift eliminated—a deletion which we shall see in Chapter 17 can seriously compromise the accuracy of the lift—but the downward and backward movement of the swing, when it is finally made, crosses the upward and forward movement of the lift. Two things take place as a result of this scissorlike action: (1) the opposing forces of lift and swing tend to cancel each other, thereby inhibiting the natural forward movement of the body in support of the swing/strike/swing, stride, and finish that is supplied when lift and swing dynamics start off in the same direction and more closely complement each other; (2) the speed of the swing is hurried because the pre-strike swing must be accelerated to catch up with a lift whose length of action has been appreciably diminished, or the lift is made higher than desirable to give the racket time to contact the ball at the proper altitude. The server will have a better understanding of these considerations after he has covered Chapters 16 and 17.

* * *

With better than two-thirds of the steps behind us, some of you may be wondering if we shall ever get around to the actual lifting and striking of the ball.

Patience, friends.

Don't sweat it.

Just hang in there.

Coming up next—Part Four and the real action.

PART FOUR

THE SERVE: PROPELLING ACTIONS

Step Twelve: The Lift (Ball)
Step Thirteen: The Swing/Strike/Swing
Step Fourteen: The Stride
Step Fifteen: The Finish

16 Step Twelve: The Lift (Ball)

There is some merit in maintaining that the tennis serve is comprised of only twelve steps—rather than fifteen—with the last identified simply as *The Propelling Action.*

Such reasoning can be pretty persuasive if one subscribes to our analysis of the serve's component parts in Chapter 4, where we directed the reader's attention to two things: (1) that in the course of making the total service act a fluent one, the actual propelling actions of head, body, arms, and legs, if properly coordinated, meld the actual service delivery into a single, smooth, well-timed operation; (2) that most of these propelling actions are complementally supporting to a marked degree, in that either individually or in tandem, they help start, direct, sustain, and even increase the momentum of another or several others—often in a reciprocal manner.

This last point will become particularly apparent later in the present chapter and the ones immediately following. To cite several specific examples, it will be demonstrated that: (1) the movements of the lift and pre-strike swing supplement and balance each other; (2) the upward movement of the lift helps unlock the slightly upward sweep of the pre-strike swing; (3) the forward action of the pre-strike swing initiates the stride, which, in turn, gives extra propulsion to the strike; (4) the strike accelerates the stride and gives thrust to the post-strike swing; and (5) the swing/strike/swing and stride combine to aid the execution of the finish.

In light of these and other similarly indicative considerations, only one conclusion can be drawn: lacking a harmonization of the propelling actions, all of the preparatory measures and preliminary motions can go for naught—with the end result an always unreliable and usually unsatisfactory service delivery.

Even though there's a need not only for coordination but synchronization because so many of these several physical movements are not entirely sequential but frequently overlapping, we have decided it is preferable to espouse four propelling actions rather than one. In doing so we are making a considerable concession to the "unity" position by compounding the swing and strike in Chapter 17 in recognition of their unusually close association.

We hope our judgment is sound despite some obvious difficulties.

On the face of it, for instance, dividing to conquer is bound to make our task of verbal exposition somewhat more complicated. We will be unable to finish the description of any one propelling action without beginning the description of one or more of the others. And, as indicated earlier, the weaving together of related subject matter will see our cross-reference frequency even more pronounced in this and the next three chapters than any other place in the book.

But if we are going to give our topic the proper amount of emphasis and the optimum clarity of thought—risking, it is true, some awkwardness and redundancy in style and expression—we feel it best to treat each of these propelling actions separately and in that order which makes the best sense.

And so, after a slight detour of rationalization, we are ready at last to tackle the most exacting step in the tennis serve—the lift of the ball.

As the action that most readily qualifies as the serve's pièce de résistance, the lift merits a continuing emphasis which might best be voiced with a conjunction of the following two thoughts: at the beginning of the chapter we pointed out that the preparatory measures and preliminary motions can go for naught if the propelling actions are not properly coordinated; in the balance of the chapter we shall show that no matter how well the propelling actions are coordinated, the results can be severely compromised, if not nullified, should the lift be either poorly made or not made as intended.

The lift occurs immediately after the server has maintained the final stand-up recovery position for a second or two, while holding his breath at the conclusion of the first contrived exhalation (see Chapter 15).

Positioning the fingers gently around the ball, the server begins the lifting action while the ball is adjacent to—but not touching—the racket's strings at shoulder level directly over the front knee, with the ball palm turned toward the server's face (see Chapters 14 and 15). There are two movements involved in the lift—each in basically opposite directions: a downward movement that starts with the beginning of the second contrived inhalation and parallels the downward movement of the pre-strike swing; an upward movement that sees the ball leave the lifting fingers at the end of the second contrived inhalation and parallels the backward and slightly upward sweep of the pre-strike swing (see Chapters 11 and 17). No break occurs between the two movements, i.e., both maintain an even pace throughout that is smooth, continuous, and unhurried—though not so slow that it loses momentum in the process.

In the downward movement, the hand fingering the ball, with wrist firm, descends to a position about a foot above the knee of the front leg, straightening the arm as it does so. No ball contact is made with the racket or racket arm while both arms are lowered simultaneously (see Chapter 17). And the body weight remains on the back foot, which is solidly braced on the ground, with the front heel slightly raised (see Chapter 15).

In the upward movement, with wrist continuing firm, the ball is lifted toward the server's selected overhead target for the strike, with the ball continuing to rise after leaving the fingers at about head level. The ball is elevated with enough momentum to permit its climb to the maximum height at which the server can make racket contact while standing on his toes and reaching for the ball in the manner required by the kind of serve he intends to deliver (see Chapter 17). During this movement, the ball arm remains straight, continues rising to a full extension after the ball leaves the fingers and automatically returns to the server's side in a manner that will best help him sustain body balance. As soon as the ball is in the air, the body weight shifts forward and upward from back foot to front foot as the server rises slightly on his toes, the stride gets under way, and the pre-strike swing moves toward the strike (see Chapters 17 and 18).

To help make his lifts properly the server should be aware of several additional key matters.

First of all, he should remember that when the upward movement is made, it must be literally a lift—and a lift only—to minimize ball spin (see Chapter 14). Further, he should recognize that the height of the ball's rise should be wholly dependent on the speed of the entire arm's elevation, i.e., no extra impetus must be added to the ball's ascent by a vertical snap of the wrist or a vertical pop of the ball with a flick of the fingers. Actually, the ball is being cupped so gently in the fingers that the momentum of the rising arm allows it to take off by itself and continue toward its apex on its own.

Second, he should recognize that it is the skill required to establish and maintain the correct elevation as well as control the intended direction that makes the lift so difficult to perform well. With this in mind, he should make particularly sure that the ball rises to a height no less than the level where he intends to make racket contact. Any elevation that is much less can cramp the swing and cut down the size of the vertical angle that can be drawn from the striking point in the air to the two ground points that represent the extreme limits measuring the depth of the potential target area—thus increasing the chances that the serve will either be netted or travel beyond the receiver's service line. Any elevation that is much more may require the server to contact a ball that is dropping too fast to strike accurately with any consistency. And any elevation that is either much less or much more can thwart the timing of all the other propelling actions. This does not mean, however, that the server should make a fetish of trying to contact the ball within extremely narrow limits, such as attempting to lift it to that height that will permit the server to contact it at the exact moment between its rise and fall—when it is motionless—as recommended by some tennis instructors. When this happens, the server is likely to concentrate on a refinement which is not that critical and may detract attention from other elements in the serve that are far more important. But it does mean that the server should continuously strive for the right height with his lift—this side, of course, of letting it get him down if it isn't perfect.

Third, he should appreciate that if the front foot is properly positioned no more than an inch or two behind the base line, the body weight maintained on the back foot until the ball leaves the lifting hand, and the ball arm held relatively straight during the upward motion of the lift, the ball is most likely to be directed in a path that cants sufficiently forward to permit the server to strike it where racket contact should be made—as much as several feet inside the server's court. This differential in distance is primarily dependent on: (1) the height of the server's reach, and (2) the way the server's body is turned after the lift is made, i.e., the more he ends up facing the net, the more he must reach inside his base line to contact the ball, and the more he ends up facing the side line, the less he must reach inside his base line to contact the ball. More on this in Chapter 17.

Fourth, he should realize that his eyes should be fastened on the ball beginning no later than the time it leaves his fingers and continuing until racket contact takes place. Failure to do so can cause many unnecessary service errors.

As indicated in Chapters 7 and 10, the position in the air toward which the lift can be most easily directed may relate to the stance that is assumed; and the way the server can most productively stroke the ball when the strike is made should relate primarily to the way the ball is actually lifted.

A close look at the interrelationship of these three variables—particularly the key middle position of the lift—can be a real eye-opener.

First of all, since the stance must precede the lift, and the lift must precede the strike, a server is bound to benefit if he predetermines all three at the time he makes the *decisions* (see Chapter 7).

Second, when the server decides to assume the most useful stance, or deliver the lift that is the easiest to make, or strike the ball with his most productive stroke, each of these options requires a set mix of the other two if optimum results are to be realized the highest percentage of the time.

Third, when the most useful stance is not assumed—primarily through carelessness—or the easiest lift not made—most often through lack of talent—there is always a single mix of both with the strike that can best compensate for the fact that the most favorable combination of variables is not available when the ball is struck.

Fourth, the better server is the one who knows how to make an instantaneous adjustment of the mix of stance, lift, and strike when either the stance is poor, or the lift does not come off as planned. Since the stance is a static set and, therefore, comparatively easy to regulate and control, this usually means adjusting the strike to accommodate a lift that has been bungled, or executed differently than planned. It is the ability to make this adjustment almost automatically that separates the men from the boys in serving. Further, this talent will only be found in those who are fully aware of the interdependence of the lift and the impact it has on so many of the service components—particularly the other propelling actions.

Fifth, despite these apparent limitations, any good stance, satisfactory lift, or properly performed strike is able, if necessary, to accommodate any mix of the other two with surprisingly few exceptions. The top professional players actually take advantage of this fact. Their propelling actions leading up to the strike are often so similar in pattern that they can successfully mask the kinds of serves they intend to deliver until a split second before the racket actually contacts the ball.

Let's proceed next to develop this linking of stance, lift, and strike even further by filling in some likely blanks in the reader's understanding with a series of questions and answers.

Q. What is the range of usable stances a server can assume?

A. The range of usable stances employed by most servers limits the forward direction of the back foot to a position pointing at ninety degrees, and the front foot to positions pointing at angles between forty-five and ninety degrees, to the intended flight of the serve (see Chapter 10).

Q. What is the range of usable lifts a server can make?

A. Theoretically, the range of usable lifts a server can make is limited only by the number of directions the ball can be elevated from any stance that will permit it to be struck inside the server's base line to a distance that can often measure several feet. Realistically, this range forms an arc of lifts in a plane that faces the service target in the receiver's court—fanning out radially and upward from a position approximately a foot above the server's front—or ball—knee, where the lift's upward movement begins, and encompassing a dial position that measures roughly from 11:30 to 12:15 o'clock for right-handed servers (see Figure 6). A mirror image of Figure 6 will show that this dial position measures roughly from 11:45 to 12:30 o'clock for left-handed servers.

Q. What is the range of usable strokes a server can strike?

A. Most tennis instruction covers three service strokes—the flat, the slice, and the American twist. In this book we will include a fourth—the top spin. Actually, all usable service strokes fit into a spectrum encompassing countless variations of the way the frame can be angled and the racket propelled for contact with the ball—starting at one end of the lifting arc where the slice and flat can be most effectively struck, and moving gradually through the top spin to finish at the other end where the American twist can be most effectively struck (see Figure 6). How these service strokes are made will be discussed in Chapter 17.

Q. What is the most useful stance an average server can assume?

A. The most useful stance an average server can assume is probably the most widely used, i.e., the one in which the front foot is pointed diagonally forward at a forty-five degree angle, and the back foot pointed at a ninety degree angle, to the direction of the intended flight of the serve (see Figures 4 and 5). This stance is as comfortable as any and can best accommodate the complete range of usable lifts that can be made with the ball and, consequently, the complete range of usable strokes that can be executed with the strike.

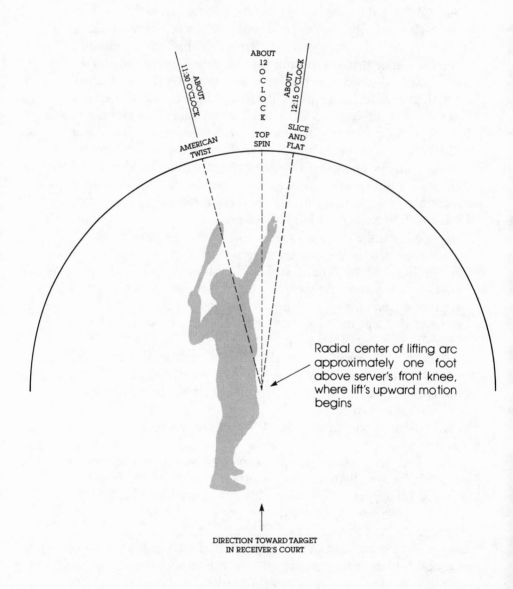

RIGHT-HANDED SERVER'S
PREFERRED LIFTING DIRECTIONS

ABOUT
12
O
C
L
O
C
K

ABOUT
11:30 O'CLOCK

ABOUT
12:15 O'CLOCK

AMERICAN
TWIST

TOP
SPIN

SLICE
AND
FLAT

Radial center of lifting arc approximately one foot above server's front knee, where lift's upward motion begins

DIRECTION TOWARD TARGET
IN RECEIVER'S COURT

FIGURE 6

Q. What is the easiest lift an average server can make?

A. The lift is crucial for two reasons: (1) it has the most dramatic effect on the serve's success or failure of any of the service components; (2) it is the most difficult service movement to perform well. As a consequence, no lift is really easy. No matter how or from what position it is made, it involves controlling the coordination of such variables as the direction in which the lift of the ball should go, the timing and momentum of the ball's rise through the air, the minimization of rotation once the ball leaves the lifting hand, and the height to which the ball should be elevated— each of which is subject to appreciable error in its own right.

We can, however, speak relatively. In that vein, the easiest lift an average server can make is probably the one in which the ball is raised in the same plane and direction as both the intended flight of the serve and the forward movement of the stride (see Chapter 18)—i.e., toward the twelve o'clock dial position (see Figure 6). The reason is that this is the one and only time when the server can simultaneously line up the vertical path of the elevating action with both: (1) the racket frame's starting position in the air, where the lift begins, and (2) the service target in the receiver's court—and also observe exactly how the arm should fall and rise toward the flight of the ball. This advantage is simply not available when the server makes any other lift, since in fronting the vertical path of the elevating movement he will always be looking away from the service target to some degree.

Q. When the average server assumes the most useful stance and makes the easiest lift, what stroke can produce optimum results the highest percentage of the time?

A. When the average server assumes the most useful stance and makes the easiest lift, he can probably realize the best payoff over the long haul if the ball is struck with a top spin stroke. We shall talk more about this in Chapter 17.

Q. What stroke when struck by an average server produces the most winners when the ball lands in play?

A. When the ball lands in play, the stroke producing the most winners for an average server is probably the flat service, a delivery that is made in conjunction with the most natural throwing motion and one that relies on speed rather than spin. Unfortunately, however—as we shall see in Chapter 17—only the taller players can use it to full advantage.

To summarize: once the average server assumes a stance, there is a particular lift that can realize optimum results the highest percentage of the time; and once he makes a particular lift, there is a particular service stroke that can realize optimum results the highest percentage of the time. As for the beginner, let it be said that once he is familiar with the elements of the swing/strike/swing, as covered in Chapter 17, he should be even more aware of this conjunction, better able to recognize the preferred alternatives when stance and lift—particularly the lift—go astray, and better acquainted with how the serve can become the offensive weapon it is intended to be.

Before we end this chapter, let us offer two more suggestions about the lift that should be helpful.

Many beginners—and even some finished players—find that associating the lift and related propelling actions with a "one(drop hands)-two(lift ball and racket)-three(strike ball)," or similar type of mental count, can help improve the timing of their service deliveries, particularly when synchronization of these movements is shaky because the actions do not seem natural. If such be the case, the server should be sure that if he is dimensioning the tempo of his breathing, the second contrived respiration (see Chapter 11), which brackets the "lift through strike" actions, is properly coordinated as well. After a period of time, it is entirely possible that correct breathing can actually replace the need for a special cadence. Such an option must, of course, remain a matter of personal choice.

Even more important is a correct understanding of how to handle or reconcile the intended stroke with the misguided lift.

If the lift is so far out of line that it cannot be struck effectively with any stroke—something that can happen more frequently than most players realize—remember that there is no penalty if you let it go unstruck and start all over. Too many servers tend to forgo this option. Some do not recognize how bad many of their lifts really are. Others are too lazy and occasionally even too embarrassed to repeat the process. Whatever the reason, there is little excuse for the unfortunate consequences that usually result.

If, however, the lift rises to a position in the air that is different than intended but still within the rough limitations of the hitting zone as defined by the lifting arc shown in Figure 6, strike it with the most effective stroke for that position—the way a good batter in baseball hits to right or left field, depending on where the ball crosses the strike zone.

This is the flexibility a player requires to be a successful server.

If you are able to adapt in this way, your serve is bound to improve measureably.

17 Step Thirteen: The Swing/ Strike/Swing

It's a doctrine supported by any good golf professional: to realize maximum distance with his drive a player should swing through the ball and accelerate the club head at impact.

Though not as widely acclaimed, the same principle holds true in tennis: to realize maximum speed or spin—or both—with his service a player should swing through the ball and accelerate the racket's striking face at impact.

With this as a starting point, it follows that the swing and strike in the tennis serve can best be performed if completely integrated— our primary reason for combining them as a single propelling action. Further, by calling Step Thirteen the *swing/strike/swing*, it can also be demonstrated that the swing actually brackets the strike, i.e., that there is both a pre-strike swing and post-strike swing. And, finally, by wrapping the strike in a swing sandwich, we hope to persuade our readers that when racket meets ball, it is primarily a sweeping action moving through the contact, rather than a colliding action terminating with the contact. This last explains why we have been careful throughout the book to specify that, in serving, the racket strikes the ball rather than hits it—a terminology refinement which, to our way of thinking, places more emphasis on movement and less on encounter.

However one may view the matter, the swing and strike are the most closely allied components in the tennis serve. Were we not fully convinced that detailing these two actions deserves individual identification and isolated treatment, we might very well have decided to call Step Thirteen simply the *delivery*—and let it go at that.

To give the reader a better grasp of the words describing the swing/strike/swing in this chapter we have included, for each of the four types of serves covered, two eight-frame sets of continuous motion photographs that bracket the serve's propelling actions— each set is a series of side, front, or back views depicting these actions in chronological order. While the pre-strike delivery style of a former champion like author Trabert, the model for these pictures, rests on a structure of elements that may appear identical to the naked eye (see our comments on this in Chapter 16), they can be so well-disguised that the camera often fails to supply a sharp delineation between the ways he swings at the ball for different serves. What these pix will do, however, is emphasize the fundamentals of the service action, particularly if one reads what follows first and senses what is critical to look for in the photos later.

As for our left-handed readers, a mirror to study these action photos, while a little awkward to pull off with much facility, can work. At least it should be no more difficult a learning process than what members of this minority group in reverse physical adeptness have had to face most of their lives. So what else is new?

THE PRE-STRIKE SWING. The pre-strike swing occurs immediately after the server has maintained the final stand-up recovery position for a second or two, while holding his breath at the conclusion of the first contrived exhalation (see Chapter 15).

Grasping the racket gently, but firmly, the server begins the action with the racket strings adjacent to—but not touching—the ball at shoulder level, directly over the front knee (see Chapter 16). Maintaining a continuous action throughout, the racket is guided toward the strike by a racket wrist that travels in several different directions. First, there is a *downward movement* that starts with the beginning of the second contrived inhalation and parallels the downward movement of the lift. Next, there is a *backward and slightly upward sweep* that parallels the upward movement of the lift to the point where the ball leaves the fingers at the end of the second contrived inhalation. Finally, there is an *upward and slightly forward loop*, while the ball is in the air, leading to an *upward and decidedly forward movement* toward contact with the ball, which takes place as the second contrived exhalation ends energetically in what is often an audible grunt (see Chapter 11). If the lift is made correctly, these pre-strike actions should maintain a relatively even tempo that picks up impetus just before the strike and sustains a good share of that impetus into the post-strike swing.

In the *downward movement*, and the *backward and slightly upward sweep*, the racket, following a semi-circular route, moves down past the racket foot in a backward direction and, with elbow straightening, ends up pointing away from the body, as the racket wrist initiates the arm rotation that will open the striking face of the racket to the sky. No racket contact is made with the ball or ball arm while both arms are lowered simultaneously (see Chapter 16). And the body weight remains on the back foot, which is solidly braced on the ground, with the front heel slightly raised (see Chapter 15).

In the *upward and slightly forward loop*, the racket wrist finishes opening the striking face of the racket and, following a curved path, climbs to a location behind the server's neck in a cocked posture, as a bending elbow points the racket toward the ground in what is often called the *back-scratching* position. Simultaneously, there is a shoulder turn away from the net, as the weight shifts from the back foot to the front foot and the body leans toward the net.

In the *upward and decidedly forward movement*, the racket shoulder is rotated forward as the racket is raised toward the ball, while the back foot moves ahead to initiate the stride, and the server performs the turn of the body and/or arch of the spine and/or flex in the knees that is required by the kind of serve selected for delivery—a matter we will cover further when we discuss the strike later on in this chapter. Just before the racket contacts the ball, the racket wrist uncocks and accelerates the face of the racket through the ball with a full forward snap, which causes the frame to overtake the rising arm with considerable velocity—the elbow leading the swing up and forward. Immediately prior to the strike, the ball leg is stretched to lengthen the reach; the racket elbow is straightened, as required, to lengthen either the pre-strike swing's reach or, in the case of some serves, the arc of the strike's final whip; and the server cants a good bit forward of the vertical. These last actions are timed to permit contact with the ball at a height no less than what we shall learn in the following pages is the optimum height for the kind of serve to be struck and at a distance that can often measure as much as several feet inside the base line (see Chapters 11 and 16).

Though not always recognized as such, these somewhat extraneous appearing movements of torso and legs, in balance with the propelling actions of the arms, have a genuine purpose: to furnish that rhythmic power which will best allow the full weight of the body and all of its extremities to supply extra thrust when racket contact with the ball is finally made. Toward this objective, in letting the swing start off at a rather deliberate pace that builds up to a crescendo, don't make the mistake of snapping the racket wrist too soon. It will not only inhibit the force but break up the timing of the strike.

Americans serve especially well because the physical actions involved are much like those required to throw a baseball—particularly the hurling techniques of a pitcher when a man is on base. The downward part of the server's lift and swing from the final recovery position is similar to the pitcher's *stretch;* the subsequent foot actions, arm maneuvers, body movements, and simultaneous weight shifting are basically facsimile for both; and, most important of all, the wrist snap of the racket arm when strings meet ball gives an impetus to the strike that is surprisingly comparable to the impetus to the throw a pitcher activates with a similar wrist snap of the throwing arm. Finally, the serve's upward swing combined with the post-strike swing are natural overhand actions that are much like throwing the racket at the ball, without letting go of the handle, and following through after contact in the way a pitcher follows through after releasing the ball toward the plate. The follow-through in both serving and pitching is vitally important. This is why we do not feel it wise to compare the service action with hammering a nail, an association cited by some instructors despite the fact that the latter pounding action involves a complete halt at impact—a decided flaw in the tennis serve.

Anyone who can throw a baseball with natural grace has automatically learned many of the essential elements of good service action. For those who are awkward throwers, a good way to develop the right service "feel" is to practice hurling tennis balls with a slow overhand motion at a target some twenty feet high on the blank wall of a structure some twenty feet away, starting the action with the throwing—or racket—hand well down one's back, while the ball hand points at the target, and bending forward to bring the throwing hand down to waist level in a forward sweep after the ball has been released. It can do a lot to help.

Some good servers forgo a full downward movement for the lift and the initiation of the pre-strike swing, beginning both at just above belt level; they apparently feel that starting these actions from shoulder level involves movement that is hard to justify. A few go further and see no reason for any downward movement whatsoever.

We won't knock those players who are so inclined. They have at least a debatable point—which leads to our suggesting this compromise.

Start off using the full lift and pre-strike swing. When the lift is grooved satisfactorily—and this may take some time, if it ever happens at all—switch, if this seems preferable, to the lift and pre-strike swing with the abbreviated downward movement, i.e., from the final recovery posture (see Chapter 15), move the ball and racket to the belt-high position, just above where the lift should begin its rise, and begin the synchronized downward movement of both hands from there. Or, if you wish, go the last mile and eliminate the downward movement entirely.

If, during play, the lift turns sour again, switch back to a full, or partial, lift and pre-strike swing to check out the lifting action. Return to the shorter downward movement or no downward movement only when the lift is once again in satisfactory sync.

In deciding how to handle this matter, keep the following in mind, however.

First of all, consistency in making a good lift can be improved for many when a somewhat longer downward movement precedes the upward movement toward release. Try lofting a tennis ball into a basketball hoop—gradually increasing the distance you first lower the propelling hand—and the difference in accuracy may surprise you.

Second, a somewhat longer downward movement of the racket arm at the initiation of the pre-strike swing can be just as advantageous to the server as the stretch is to the baseball pitcher when a man on base means the pitcher must dispense with the complete windup. In both cases the timing of the action, as well as the buildup in the momentum, are likely to be better controlled than from a pitcher's "set" position, i.e., with both hands starting the action from the belt—or below.

These are the kinds of things which say that serving with a full lift and full pre-strike swing has a lot going for it. Its significance in the case of any given player, however, can only be determined by what that player decides is best for him.

The Strike. Up till now we've been pretty extravagant about the criticality of the lift. And we certainly do not intend to back off from such a position at this time.

But if the lift is the pièce de résistance as the principal key to service proficiency, the strike is assuredly the sine qua non in measuring service success. However one may rationalize the matter, the server's primary purpose is to put the ball in play in such a way that the receiver either cannot get it back or returns it so weakly that the server has no difficulty ending the point with a winner. While the first twelve-plus service steps can, and must, lay the necessary groundwork—with the lift in the most strategic position of all—none of them can guarantee that an effective delivery will be made. This can only happen if the strike is properly executed.

The strike is the only propelling action whose principal purpose—moving the ball—is realized instantaneously. In addition, it: (1) maximizes the momentum of the pre-strike swing as it initiates the momentum of the post-strike swing—bridging the two; and (2) furnishes the chief energizing force required to pivot the body at the waist until the server is facing the net, propel the upper torso and stride of the rear—or racket—leg across the service line, and set up the finish.

To make the strike work, one must be sure the racket is so angled that the combination of a snap of the wrist and follow-through of the arm will: (1) allow the racket's face to contact the ball with good velocity at a position on the strings about halfway between the frame sides and slightly more than halfway between the neck and frame top; (2) deliver the serve in the desired direction with the correct spin; and (3) permit the subsequent propelling actions to proceed properly. In choosing the stroke for the strike, keep the following in mind: the more the racket face is directed toward the service court target when ball contact is made, the faster the ball will travel, the less it will revolve, the less abnormal its height of bounce, and the less errant its direction of bounce away from the line of flight when it lands in the opponent's court; conversely, the more the racket face is directed away from the service court target when ball contact is made, the slower the ball will travel, the more it will revolve, the more its height of bounce may vary, and the more its direction of bounce may swerve away from the line of flight when it lands in the opponent's court.

In the process of grooving the cadence of a reliable swing, it is best to gain service control before trying to develop service intensity. Remember that the velocity with which the ball travels is by no means the sole standard of service quality. In truth, a delivery based on raw power alone is seldom a server's most dependable winner. This explains why the seasoned professional alternates speed and spin or—better yet—uses a varying mixture of both for certain types of delivery. It is particularly good strategy for a player to employ a spin delivery if an opponent is returning a speed delivery with consistent success—or vice versa.

What may be surprising to many is that if the type of delivery selected is made in accordance with the clock positions shown for the lift in Figure 6, the pre-strike swing actions are basically the same for all service strokes—with the following two exceptions.

First of all, in stretching for the ball, the server should be aware that if a fast slice or flat serve is to be struck, the racket arm and racket are pretty much at full extension from the base of the armpit, as the ball is contacted forward of the base line. If a top spin or American twist serve is to be struck, however, a shift in the position of the racket frame, to a location above or beyond the server's head on the ball-shoulder side, sees the ball contacted somewhat below full extension with an upward sweeping motion that continues rising until the racket arm finally reaches full extension. This adjustment in swing action allows the server to impart the overspin necessary to make these serves arc in such a way that the ball will bounce in the manner desired within a target range that is safely in play. More later on how the racket is slanted to meet the ball for different serves.

Second, the body turn at the waist produced by the pre-strike swing of the slice or flat is somewhat more pronounced than that produced by the top spin and significantly more than that produced by the American twist. On the other hand, these latter two high-bounding deliveries require the server to direct the racket not only forward toward the net but upward toward the sky. This means that to be performed properly the top spin and American twist must generate a backward arch of the spine and flexing of the knees. These postures permit a subsequent unwinding of the torso and straightening of the legs to supply extra impetus to the strike, as the body recovers from its bent position, extends upward on its ball toes, and inclines forward of the vertical. All of these actions are particularly arduous when striking an American twist—a fact that goes far to explain why this delivery is the most difficult for most players to perform consistently well.

In the next several paragraphs we shall describe four service strokes—the slice, flat, top spin, and American twist. While there is an isolated and arbitrarily dimensioned limitation for each, it should be recalled from Chapter 16 that all preferred service deliveries for different lifts fit into a spectrum that requires a gradual change in racket face angle at ball contact as one moves across the arc of lifts illustrated in Figure 6. This means that the strokes selected are really only bench marks, and that there are an infinite number of shaded variations in between.

The Slice. The slice serve is most effectively struck by the right-hander at the lifting arc's dial position of about 12:15 (see Chapter 16 and Figure 6). If properly executed, it gives the ball a propulsion that is diagonally forward and downward toward the ball-arm side of the receiver's court, and a rotation similar to a hook in golf, or a pitcher's outcurve in baseball. This is accomplished by: (1) contacting the ball with a fully extended racket arm and racket stretching in a fairly straight line into the court at impact, the racket's striking surface turned slightly away from the intended flight of the service toward the ball-arm side of the receiver's court; and (2) letting the swing actions immediately surrounding the actual strike: (a) originate from a posture that sees no arch of the spine or flex in the knees and (b) end up with the body facing the net. When racket meets ball, the strings not only propel it in the desired direction but do so with a brushing action that moves the racket face, as viewed by the server, up and around the ball at approximately a 2 o'clock location and imparts a rotation that is fundamentally a clockwise side spin with a top spin modification. This causes the ball to curve significantly across the court in front of the server in the same direction he rotates his body toward the net. When the ball lands, it bounces relatively low in a skidding fashion that can be hard to handle, the flight arc continuing basically to maintain its original bearing.

For most players the slice is the most natural service stroke to use. If struck correctly, it produces the fastest curve in combination with the most forward thrust of all the spin serves and is most effective on a fast court surface because the ball will skid even more quickly and in a still wider curve. The slice is particularly effective when struck by the right-handed server against the left-handed receiver—or vice versa—since in both instances the ball will, in many cases, move away from the receiver on what is normally his weaker side, the backhand. It can also, on occasion, make it awkward for any receiver to execute a good return by veering into one side of his body, cramping his first ground stroke and often forcing either an error or weak return that is easy for the server to put away.

The slice does have several potential problems, however. For one thing, its relatively flat trajectory makes it harder for the ball to clear the net and still remain in play—particularly when the server is a shorter player. For another, it is the most difficult serve to strike to a receiver's backhand if both players strike the ball from the same side.

The Flat. The flat serve is most effectively struck by the right-hander at the lifting arc's dial position of about 12:15 (see Chapter 16 and Figure 6). If properly executed, it gives the ball maximum forward propulsion and no rotation of any real consequence. This is accomplished by: (1) contacting the ball with a fully extended racket arm and racket stretching in close to a straight line into the court at impact, the racket's striking surface, for the most part, directly facing the intended flight of the service; and (2) letting the swing actions immediately surrounding the actual strike: (a) originate from a posture that sees no arch of the spine or flex in the knees and (b) end up with the body facing the net. When racket meets ball, the strings not only propel it in the desired direction but do so with full force, as the server performs an action that looks somewhat similar to the way a baseball pitcher delivers an overhand fast ball. This causes the ball to travel in a relatively straight line across the court in front of the server, as he rotates his body toward the net. When the ball lands, it bounces in the direction of the line of flight.

In executing a flat serve, remember that the important thing is to strike the ball *hard*. Don't worry if you put a slight spin on the delivery. It is impossible not to do so.

For many players, the flat is not only the fastest but can be the most productive serve that can be struck. It should only be used for the first serve, however. To help understand why, consider the following.

In Chapter 16 it was brought out that the lower the elevation of the lifted ball at racket contact, the less the vertical angle that can be

The Slice

Racket and ball
lowered from about
shoulder level . . .
Front foot behind
base line . . . Eyes
on target

Arms raised
in unison

Lift directed
with full
extension
toward 12:15
target

Eyes on ball . . .
Rotating arm
starts opening . .
racket striking . .
face toward sky

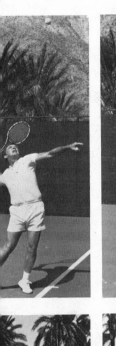

Start of
weight shift
forward

"Scratch back"
with racket and
start body turn
toward net

Prepare to
accelerate
racket
through ball
well inside
base line

Post-strike
swing helps
turn body
toward net

The Flat

Weight on back
foot . . . Front heel
slightly raised . . .
Downward movement
of arms already
under way

Upward
movement
of lift with
wrist firm

Lift directed
with full
extension
toward 12:15
target

Bend racket
elbow . . . Raise
back heel
slightly

...e-strike
...wing initiates
...ride

"Throw" racket
at ball with
full racket arm
extension . . .
Ball leg
stretched to
lengthen reach

Continue stride
well inside
base line
(See Chap. 18)

Complete stride
with weight
returned to
racket foot
(See Chap. 18)

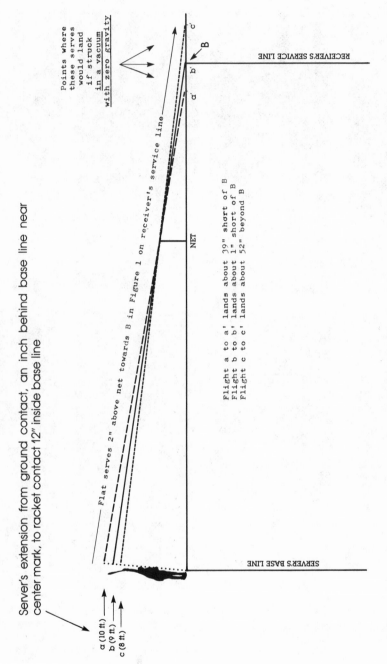

FLAT SERVE FLIGHTS
FROM DIFFERENT HEIGHTS

Server's extension from ground contact, an inch behind base line near center mark, to racket contact 12" inside base line

Flat serves 2" above net towards B in Figure 1 on receiver's service line

a (10 ft.) ⟶
b (9 ft.) ⟶
c (8 ft.) ⟶

Points where these serves would land if struck in a vacuum with zero gravity

RECEIVER'S SERVICE LINE

NET

SERVER'S BASE LINE

Flight a to a' lands about 39" short of B
Flight b to b' lands about 1" short of B
Flight c to c' lands about 52" beyond B

FIGURE 7

drawn from the striking point in the air to the two ground points that represent the extreme limits measuring the depth of the potential target area—thus making it less likely that the ball will land in the receiver's court as required. This is especially handicapping to the flat serve.

Figure 7 illustrates this point more exactly by exaggerating the problem. It does so by showing where flat serves would land near the receiver's service line from different heights of racket contact if the server struck the ball in a vacuum with zero gravity and: (1) stood about an inch behind his base line in a position nearest his center mark; (2) contacted the ball some twelve inches inside his backcourt; (3) cleared the net by approximately two inches with a delivery that moved toward B in Figure 1, the point in the receiver's service court where service line and center service line intersect.

G force and air friction are, of course, always very much in the picture. What may be surprising is that the variations in horizontal deflection caused by the "drop" and "drag" of these constraints—especially on post-net as compared with pre-net flight—tend to balance out when measured against variations in service propulsion.

Let us demonstrate what we mean.

No matter how much control he may have of his deliveries, a server cannot expect that he will consistently clear the net by as little as two inches with his flat serves. This makes it unlikely that the ball will land in play at, or in front of, point B and decreases the probability that Figure 7 gives a reasonably accurate picture of what may be expected if the other limitations hold as defined.

On the other hand, caution, fatigue—or both—will rarely see the server uniformly strike his flat serve with the speed that is required to make it the offensive weapon it could be. The slower the flight, the greater the diversionary effect of gravity and air. This increases the chance the ball will land in play at or in front of point B and increases the probability that Figure 7 gives a reasonably accurate picture of what may be expected within the limitations defined—even if the net clearance is quite a bit more than two inches.

The bottom line is a sort of Mexican standoff that gives the significance of Figure 7 more true-life credence than one may be inclined to recognize at first glance.

In studying Figure 7, don't overlook the fact that the server's racket contact is made some twelve inches inside his backcourt and his front—or ball—foot is positioned about an inch behind his base line. This means that we are really talking about "extension from ground contact of front foot to racket contact"—a distance that is somewhat more than "height of racket contact above ground."

However one may look at it, Figure 7 does give a pretty accurate relative picture of the effect of the height of the server's racket contact on the delivery of a fast flat serve that is struck hard enough to be productive. Normally, a server approximately five feet eight inches tall can rise on his toes and contact the ball with his racket at the right spot on the strings via an extension of about nine feet from the ground contact of the front—or ball—foot. Figure 7 shows this to be the extension from which a flat serve will land slightly more than an inch short of point B in Figure 1 if struck within the limitations defined. The greater the extension above nine feet, the greater will be the distance short of point B where a similarly struck flat serve will land (about thirty-nine inches from an extension of ten feet, for example). The less the extension below nine feet, the greater will be the distance beyond point B where a similarly struck flat serve will land (about fifty-two inches from an extension of eight feet, for example).

From this we can conclude that nine feet is roughly the break-even extension above which a sufficiently fast flat serve can be struck with reasonable expectancy of success, but below which the odds are stacked against a favorable outcome for such a delivery. This says that in those cases when the lift for a flat serve does not seem to have risen high enough to permit the necessary extension, do one of three things: (1) let it drop unstruck; (2) strike it with less velocity and hope for the best; or (3) strike it with a spin delivery.

The preceding analysis makes a strong case for those who profess that relatively few women players are tall enough to strike a fast flat serve consistently well. And it gives a lot of support to the suggestion that most women players should learn to use some sort of spin serve as their basic service tool.

By the same token, this analysis also indicates that some one of these fine days a seven-foot human skyscraper with the speed and reflexes of a basketball guard—a not unlikely combination in the amazing youth of the eighties—will have taken up tennis at an early age and developed into a real champion because of his devastating cannonball serve. A Stan Smith "plus," in a sense.

The Top Spin. The top spin serve is most effectively struck by either the right-hander or left-hander at the lifting arc's dial position of about twelve o'clock (see Chapter 16 and Figure 6). If properly executed, it gives the ball forward propulsion and a rotation similar to a topped drive in golf, or a pitcher's sinker in baseball. This is accomplished by: (1) canting the racket frame above the server's head in such a way that the long axis of the racket handle assumes a position that is almost horizontal to the ground, the racket's striking surface directly facing the intended flight of the serve; (2) contacting the ball with the racket arm extending in a fairly straight line into the court following impact; and (3) letting the swing actions immediately surrounding the actual strike: (a) originate from a posture that sees a slight arch of the spine and flex in the knees and (b) end with the body facing the net. When racket meets ball, the strings not only propel it in the desired direction but do so with a power-sweeping movement that moves the racket face, as viewed by the server, up and over the ball via pretty much a full stretch in approximately a twelve o'clock direction. This causes the ball to move straight ahead in a tumbling spin that generates a decidedly dipping action as it travels across the court in front of the server, while there is a slight rotation of his body toward the net. When the ball lands, it bounces high but does not veer appreciably from the line of flight.

Use of the top spin gives the server a number of advantages. First of all, when struck hard, its plunging action has a greater margin of safety than the flat and makes it less likely to take off and fly out of court than the slice. Second, its higher bounce toward the back-court will often keep the receiver nearer his base line and compli-cate his making a forcing return even when the top spin lands closer to the net than the server had intended. Both of these features can make the top spin a good choice for the second serve. In addition—unlike the slice or flat—the top spin should be able to be struck as

The Top Spin

Body relaxed . . .
Racket grasped
gently but
firmly . . . Arms
straighten as they
continue descent
in unison

Lift and
pre-strike swing
supplement and
balance
each other

Lift directed
with full
extension
toward twelve
o'clock target

Upward/slightly
forward racket
loop . . . Racket
shoulder turn
begins

Racket wrist
stays cocked . . .
Spine slightly
arched

Elbow leads
swing toward
strike . . .
Racket wrist
snaps forward

Stride gives
strike extra
propulsion

Complete
post-strike
swing with
racket pointing
at backstop

effectively by the shorter as by the taller player. Its longer flight through the air after its bounce can also give the server more time to advance to the net when the strike places the ball deep to the receiver's weak side.

The top spin has several disadvantages. Its higher and longer bounce can give an opponent more time to make a return than the slice or flat. And, the need for the server to exercise an arch of the spine and flex in the knees during the pre-strike swing can be tiring for all but the younger players if used with too much regularity. In this connection, recognize, too, the additional exertion required to achieve ball spin, which is generated by an upward sweep caused by a tandem of wrist, arm, shoulder, and body actions—not simply by a modification in the angle at which the strings meet the ball. Further, these actions must be made in unison, i.e., if the shoulder rotates or the body bends toward the strike before the arm rises and the wrist is snapped, the swing loses much of its power.

The American Twist. The American twist serve is most effectively struck by the right-hander at the lifting arc's dial position of about 11:30 (see Chapter 16 and Figure 6). If properly executed, it gives the ball a propulsion that is diagonally forward and upward toward the racket-arm side of the receiver's court and a rotation quite similar to the slice—a fact that may surprise a number of our readers. This is accomplished by: (1) canting the racket frame above the ball shoulder in such a way that the long axis of the racket handle assumes a position that is even more horizontal to the ground than the top spin, the racket's striking surface turned slightly away from the intended flight of the service toward the racket-arm side of the receiver's court, (2) contacting the ball with the racket arm extending in a fairly straight line into the court at impact; and (3) letting the swing actions immediately surrounding the actual strike: (a) originate from a somewhat contorted body posture that sees a decided arch of the spine and flex in the knees and (b) end up with the body facing the net. When racket meets ball, the strings not only propel it toward a location in the receiver's court slightly on the racket-arm side of the intended target but do so with a power-sweeping movement that moves the racket face, as viewed by the server, up and over the ball via pretty much a full stretch in approximately a seven o'clock to two o'clock direction. This imparts a tumbling action to the ball that is fundamentally a top spin with a clockwise side spin modification. While the ball starts off toward the racket-arm side of the target, its side spin causes it to end up curving back toward the target, as the server faces the net. When the ball lands, it bounces high and veers in varying degrees toward the racket-arm side of the opponent's court.

In using the American twist, the server finds it gives him a decided edge in the fact that its high bounce that swerves off line can disturb an opponent's timing and—far more than the top spin— complicate a receiver's making a forcing return, even when the ball lands closer to the net than the server had intended. It is most productive on a slow surface, which increases its gripping action and makes the ball bounce higher and more off to one side. This makes the American twist an excellent choice for the second serve, once its rather tricky technique has been mastered. It is particularly effective when the server and receiver swing from the same side, since in both instances the ball will, in many cases, move away from the receiver on what is normally his weaker side, the backhand. It can also, on occasion, make it awkward for any receiver to execute a good return by veering into one side of his body, cramping his first ground stroke, and often forcing either an error or weak return that is easy for the server to put away. In addition—like the top spin— the American twist should be able to be struck as effectively by the shorter as by the taller player. And its somewhat more leisurely flight through the air—both before and after its bounce—normally gives the server all the time he needs should he decide to advance to the net.

It won't take the server long to discover that the American twist can also pose a lot of problems. Of all the service strokes we shall cover, it is not only the slowest traveling, but the most difficult for the average player to strike with any consistent success, since it can easily be mishit so badly that it either goes way out of court or becomes a setup because its poorly managed spin—like that involved with a pitcher's hanging curve—does not allow it to break sufficiently down and into the court to produce a lopsided bounce.

The American Twist

Shoulder-width stance . . . Ball cupped in digit tips . . . Arms end drop from start position and separate

Lift helps unlock pre-strike swing

Lift directed with full extension toward 11:30 target

Body somewhat contorted with spine arched and knees flexed

oward/decidedly
rward racket
ovement . . .
acket arm
balance pole"
ction helps
quilibrium
ee Chap. 18)

Straighten spine
and incline body
toward net as
racket sweeps up
and across ball
toward racket-
arm side of
receiver's court

Racket leg
swing forward
helps turn
body toward
net

End stride and
post-strike
swing ready to
charge net or
step back
across base line
(See Chap. 19)

Further, it is even more exhausting to use with any appreciable frequency than the top spin, because it involves a far more difficult conjunction of wrist, arm, shoulder, and body actions in generating the proper spin with the upward sweep. Finally, the arching of the spine, if improperly coordinated, can not only inhibit the smooth conjunction that must be made with the subsequent stride and finish but injure the lower back. To help alleviate these several body stresses and strains some players find it best to take a stance with the front foot either perpendicular to the intended flight of the serve before the service action begins, or placed in such a position as a consequence of a pivoting rotation on the toe just before the racket contacts the ball.

Any player can eventually learn from the experience gained through trial and error or just plain happenstance that he is likely to do better by making a slight adjustment in one or more of his propelling movements when delivering some types of serves under certain specific conditions. For example, some right-handed servers have discovered that if the ball is not tossed quite as far forward as is customary, they can expect greater success when a slice serve is directed at the right service court's side line or a hard, fast serve is directed at the left service court's side line. This may not be true for everyone, of course, and we mention it here primarily to point out that each individual must conduct his own personal experiments with various elements of the service action to determine what modifications seem to reap the most for him.

While it is obvious to most that the direction of the ball's spin determines the direction of the ball's flight, many players fail to recognize that the direction of the propulsion supplied the ball by the force of the racket contact is the chief input affecting the way a ball behaves when it lands on a court surface. They are too inclined to conclude that the spin supplied the ball by the angle of the racket contact is the major determinant in both cases.

The best way we know to dissuade them from this mistaken point of view is to compare the slice service with the American twist service. While both serves give the ball much the same rotation—the slice a side spin with top spin modification, and the American twist a top spin with side spin modification—these two types of delivery bounce in entirely dissimilar ways. The main reason is that the direction of the racket propulsion for the slice is approximately at right angles to that for the American twist, i.e., diagonally forward and downward toward the ball-arm side line for the former, and diagonally forward and upward toward the racket-arm side line for the latter. This clearly indicates that it is the propulsion—not the spin—that makes the big difference in how the ball bounces.

Not many years ago, a change in tennis rules made it legal to serve with both feet off the ground. As a result, many top-notch players make a good number of their deliveries—particularly their power first services—while their bodies are actually in the air. In understanding what they are really doing, however, it is important to recognize that a good server does not employ a "hop" to bring about greater racket arm extension at ball contact but, rather, employs such a full racket arm extension at ball contact that a "hop" results as a consequence.

The dynamics involving the "hop" being what they are, we find it difficult to advocate that stretching for the ball to this degree during the service action is really going to be that beneficial. No one can ever hope to generate maximum arm power—be it throwing, hitting, serving, or what have you—unless he can take advantage of the push-off leverage furnished by having at least one foot on the ground. A baseball pitcher would never throw effectively, or a hitter bat efficiently, should either try to do so; and the reason that Floyd Patterson, a good boxer, possessed only a mediocre knockout record can be explained in large measure, perhaps, by the fact that a number of his punches were delivered with neither foot touching the canvas.

However its value be rationalized, reaching high enough with the racket to produce a "hop" will not work for every server anyway. It adds an extra variable to the propelling actions that can interfere with the timing of the swing/strike/swing and interrupt, if not entirely negate, the stride and finish. And because it is somewhat enervating, it is apt to catch up with the server in a long match, no matter how young and strong he may be.

Our advice, then: stay on terra firma when you serve. But if you do stretch high enough to generate a "hop," be sure you land on the ball foot. Coming down on the racket foot denies you the opportunity of pushing off and accelerating the stride and impetus of the post-strike swing, as well as setting up the finish. This is a particularly severe handicap if you opt to advance to the net.

It should be clear that the several service strokes we have discussed demand a rather precise execution, which can only be developed with patient concentration and conscientious drilling. What may not be quite so evident is that they also demand a good grasp by the server of how each can be utilized to net optimum results. Meeting the first requirement has limited value without realizing the second, i.e., like the well-trained physician with little aptitude for his practice, no player can serve effectively if he merely knows how and what to perform, but doesn't know where, when, and why. Make the most of both needs, however, and things will fall in place in a hurry.

The Post-strike Swing. The post-strike swing continues the action of the strike, gives some extra momentum to the movement of the upper torso and stride of the rear—or racket—leg across the server's base line, helps rotate the body toward the net, and sets up the finish.

Termination of the post-strike swing occurs when the server's racket foot touches down in his backcourt. If a slice, flat, or top spin serve has been struck, the racket arm moves down and across the front of the ball leg, ending up with the racket pointing toward the backstop behind the server. If an American twist serve has been struck, the racket arm follows a more circuitous route, moving first across the racket leg, before making its way down and across the front of the ball leg. Swinging the racket in this wider loop that actually starts out up and away from the body helps the server recover from the arched-spine and flexed-knee positions he had assumed prior to contacting the ball.

There's nothing more to it than that.

Remember, also, that striking the serve by sweeping through the ball with the swing has several additional advantages. For one thing, it can increase the chances that the served ball will travel toward the selected target in the opponent's court. For another, in helping the server shift his weight back to the racket foot and incline his body forward, it can do much to assure that maximum power has been generated when the strings contact the ball. And for still another, in helping to pivot his body so that it is properly fronting the receiver's return, it prepares the server to shift in any direction subsequent strategy may dictate (see Chapter 19).

This has been a long chapter.

In our insistence that the swing/strike/swing must be integrated to be viewed in the right context, it is possible that we have tried to blanket too much ground simultaneously and left some of you talking to yourselves.

Actually the basic essentials can be stated in capsule form quite simply: a service delivery should not come about as the consequence of a hit but, rather, in the course of a swing that sees you accelerate the racket well beyond ball contact, with a forward snap of the wrist and stretching of the elbow after the strike takes place.

Striking the ball inside a proper swing is the big thing in the tennis serve. It's really what the service delivery is all about. Doing it effectively a good share of the time takes a lot of practice. But once you can meet the ball correctly, it's like money in the bank, i.e., it can sustain you when the rest of your game turns a little sour.

When can you consider yourself a good server? A realistic answer involves a larger dimension than some may be prepared to accept: as soon as you can consistently get better than two-thirds of your first serves in play no more than three or four feet short of the receiver's service line, using a wide assortment of different speeds and bounces directed to varying lateral locations, which keep your opponent unsure about how and where the ball will go.

The chances of your winning can be greatly enhanced if you can do so.

In a match between players of comparable abilities, statistics give considerable support to the probability that the victor is the one with the highest percentage of first service success.

18 Step Fourteen: The Stride

Of all the fifteen steps in the tennis serve, the stride may be the one which is easiest for the server to misconstrue (despite being the only actual step in the whole caboodle!). This could relate to the fact that many players suffer from the false notion that the only time a server should move across his base line with the service motion is when he intends to rush the net after he strikes the ball. As a consequence, it is important for the server to realize right off the bat that the main purpose of the stride is to help propel the ball when racket contact is made by: (1) expediting the weight shift from racket foot to ball foot and back again to racket foot; (2) generating the body momentum toward the net that powers the service delivery; and (3) accelerating the post-strike swing. That the body ends up a step nearer the net—thus making it easier for the player to advance forward to volley the service return should he so desire—is, of course, a valuable bonus but not the stride's principal raison d'être.

In simple terms, the stride is that movement of the racket foot forward from its anchored position at the end of the recovery to a position well inside the base line. While this is taking place, the ball leaves the lifting hand, the pre-strike swing continues and the strike is executed. As ball contact is made, the ball toes are raised as high as stability will permit, with the server's equilibrium helped considerably by the steadying, *balance pole* action of the empty lifting arm as it returns to the server's side. If properly executed, termination of the stride catches the player's weight on the racket foot right after the end of the post-strike swing.

Strong, flexible feet are required to make all of these things possible. Toward this end, the simple exercise of raising and lowering the body on the toes for a minute or so before play begins can help tone up the foot muscles—principally those of the metatarsus. The best way to do this is to stand on a curbing with heels overlapping the edge and arms stretched out straight ahead—the way a diver prepares for a back flip.

If you lift the ball sufficiently forward of the base line when you serve, some sort of stride is bound to take place, if for no other reason than it prevents you from falling on your face. Advance the quality of your performance a notch further, however, and take the proper stride forward, as prescribed, in coordination with the other propelling actions, every time you make a service delivery, and you'll manage a giant stride forward in the development of your serving technique.

It's a key action in assuring that racket contact with the ball is not a hit but, rather, an integral part of the swing/strike/swing.

19 Step Fifteen: The Finish

As the term used to describe the last step in the service structure, the word *finish* is really an anomaly. Certainly it contributes a good deal to making the delivery a finished product—in more ways than one. No one will argue that point. But it is far more than just an end action, since its real objective, strangely enough, is to propel the server's body into position to play the return of service that may follow. This makes its purpose less "windup" than "preparatory."

With the foregoing in mind, the server must determine how and where he should set himself for the receiver's first ground stroke. Actually, he has two basic options: (1) to stay in his backcourt, or (2) to advance toward the net. Assuming that his ground strokes and volley play are equally sound and that his opponent has no particularly glaring weaknesses, ascertaining which option to select is mainly dependent on the kind of surface on which he is playing. A clay court, which sees the ball bounce higher and more slowly, gives a receiver more time to plan and execute his return and makes a good volley by the server of that return less likely. By the same token, a concrete court, which sees the ball bounce lower and faster, gives a receiver less time to plan and execute his return and makes a good volley by the server of that return more likely—particularly when a power serve is struck that lands deep in the receiver's court. More discussion of different court surfaces will be found in Chapter 22.

If he opts to stay in his backcourt, the server, after completing the stride, should immediately move back some three feet behind his base line, continue to face his opponent and, watching him closely, crouch slightly forward in a ready position, trying to predict how the return will be made—with ball hand on racket throat and body set to move in any direction.

If he opts to advance toward the net, the server, after completing the stride, should immediately take several driving steps in a veritable charge toward his opponent, whom he watches closely throughout. As the receiver starts to make his first return, the server assumes a straddle position in preparation for making a volley—eyes on his opponent to read his intentions, ball hand on racket throat, and body crouched slightly forward, set to move in any direction. While he can resume advancing to volley the ball within a few feet of the net, should the receiver hit a weak, *sitter* return, the server should not, as a rule, volley while still moving forward. He should, of course, advance to the ideal volleying position as soon afterward as possible. When going to the net, the server should let the momentum of the swing/strike/swing initiate the movement into the forecourt in as natural a way as possible. He should never reverse the process, however, i.e., put the cart before the horse by letting the net advance rush the swing/strike/swing, thereby making it less likely that a service will go in or be good enough to warrant such an advance. Once he recognizes that sacrificing good timing in striking the ball for added quickness in reaching his forecourt is a mistake, and once he manages to arrange things mentally in the right order—and keep them there—the problem should disappear.

In the course of going to the net, the server should try to coordinate his forward movements so that when he executes his first volley from a position that may not be the best, he can step from the straddle position with the ball foot for the forehand volley or the racket foot for the backhand volley. Of course, time will not always be available to make this possible. When this is the case, it is normally preferable for a player to reach out and make the volley as best he can rather than hit a half volley—the "drop kick" shot in tennis that requires contacting the ball near the ground directly after it bounces. Like the bunker shot in golf, which can pose no particular problem for the finished player, the half volley is difficult for many to perform in other than a defensive way and should only be used by the average player when the return is not retrievable in any other way.

While the court position a server should try to reach for a volley of the service return is not a fixed objective, his chances of success are much improved if he can execute the shot from as close as possible to the ideal volleying position, i.e., some distance in advance of his service line. In doing so, he should exercise the flank-protecting *offensive* move of maintaining a middle position in the path blanketing the range covering the opponent's most likely returns—a maneuver that involves the same principles as the flank-protecting *defensive* move of the hockey goalie who decides to leave his cage to counter, as best he can, the one-on-one assault of an advancing skater. The approach, in both cases, involves the strategy of throwing an opponent off stride by suddenly introducing a scenario that forces that opponent to make a choice in a hurry between several challenging responses—a feat that can often be difficult to perform.

In singles play, a server can expect to achieve a higher percentage of favorable results if he opts to advance to the net after his first power serves, which put his opponent on the defensive, than after his second serves, which involve more spin and give his opponent a better chance to pass him with the service return. Further, quickly reaching the court position where he can execute a successful volley is not as vital when the server strikes a power delivery. There are three reasons for this: first, the power serve has a good chance of ending up an outright winner; second, it can often force an error or weak return that gives the server extra time to reach a desirable volleying position; and third, it can, on occasion, bring about a pressure return that sees the receiver, through good anticipation, make a fast, accurate ground stroke that cannot be returned by the server if he is positioned too far forward of his base line. In light of these considerations, a server may not actually need to get as far as his service line to volley the return of a power serve—with further movement dependent on how his opponent actually makes that return.

Once a server has made up his mind to rush the net and volley the receiver's return, he must stick with that decision as long as the receiver makes a return or until the serve is called a fault. Too often a player allows a last minute fear that his serve is not deep enough, or a guess that his serve will not end up in play, to quash his original plan to charge toward the net.

Learning to attack the net in the right way at the right time is primarily instinctive. But it can be improved with the help of conscientious practice and the experience of extensive play—both of which can bring a better understanding of the likely success of service returns that must cope with varying conditions of bounce and speed on various surfaces from different court locations.

With this chapter we wind up our coverage of what we believe are the major component parts in the structure of the tennis serve.

Give them a fair shake and build on them as best you can.

True—their prescribed use can never guarantee that you will always win your serve.

But should an understanding of these fifteen steps make it easier for you to score points when you do serve—and we think that's very possible for those who have not yet learned to serve as well as they might—you gotta believe!

PART FIVE

THE SERVE: OTHER SIGNIFICANT CONSIDERATIONS

20 The Serve: Doubles

Many make the pitch that tennis singles and doubles are two entirely different games. This is a defensible point of view if comparison is limited to the strategies involved in winning a match. Granted that both games employ the same tools, a facsimile scoring system, and court dimensions which are not that dissimilar in size when one considers the number of players participating, most action in doubles develops into an exchange of volleys at close quarters calling for tactics appreciably different from those used in singles.

Prior to playing the first point of a game—which sees the serve aimed at the right service court—the server, the server's partner, the receiver, and the receiver's partner will, in most cases, place themselves at or near the start positions shown in Figure 8—with the players making such adjustments as may be required to accommodate such matters as the speed of the court surface, the delivery tendencies of the server, etc. Once the service is delivered, it is the aim of the server, the receiver, and the receiver's partner to advance as soon as possible to, or near, the forward positions also shown in Figure 8—the server right after the delivery has been made, and the receiver and the receiver's partner at the first opportunity after the return has been made. A "reverse print" mirror image of this drawing will display the positions taken by the players when the serve is aimed at the left service court.

POSITIONS NORMALLY TAKEN
BY SERVING AND RECEIVING TEAMS
BEFORE AND AFTER SERVE
INTO RIGHT SERVICE COURTS

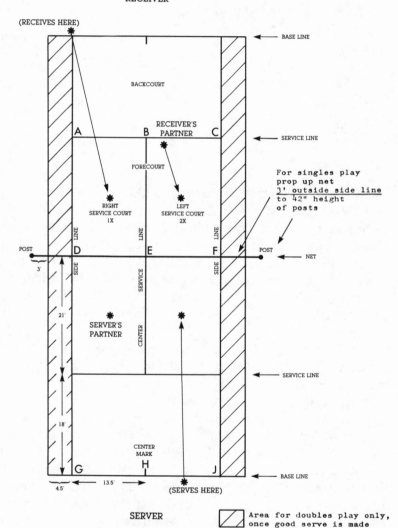

RECEIVER

SERVER

Arrows show how players should move
from their start positions
once ball is served or returned

FIGURE 8

A doubles team gains an appreciable advantage when it can realize these forecourt positions first in conjunction with an attacking shot that puts the opponents on defense. If this can be accomplished with the serve itself, the tilt takes place right off the bat. This sees the service in doubles a good deal more important in setting up an early position superiority than the service in singles.

With the above in mind, it follows that a server's success in a doubles contest depends in large measure on his satisfactorily resolving the question, "What type of serve am I going to use and where shall I direct it that will force the receiver to do no more than return a ball that is easily playable?" While the fifteen steps that make up the serve's component parts hold for both individual and team play, this means that in making the decisions discussed in Chapter 7 the options afforded the server are far more limited in doubles than in singles.

For one thing, the average server in a doubles match will normally be inclined to limit the use of a fast serve that can often be returned before he gets more than a few steps beyond his base line. On the contrary, he will tend to take off speed and add spin by making the majority of his deliveries with the higher, often irregular bouncing top spin or American twist serves that will give him plenty of time to move forward for a volley—calling on the fast slice or flat serves only when a surprise or change of pace delivery seems prudent.

For another thing, in doubles the selection of a target in the receiver's court for any serve is primarily based on "making it more difficult for the receiver to return"—with "making it easier for the server to keep the ball in play" not as pertinent a consideration. This makes placing the first serve in play even more significant in team than in individual competition.

Generally speaking, the serve in doubles should land deep on the receiver's weak side—more often than not toward his backhand. Further, while directing the serve toward the side line can be useful, it is not an option employed as much as in singles because it widens the span, and it splits the cohesion of the serving team's lateral defense by opening up the server's court and giving the receiver the option of either returning the ball down the alley, or through the center, or at a severe angle across the front of the forecourt.

Serving directly at the receiver can be very profitable in doubles if not employed to excess. An occasional fast serve to the receiver's strength, to counter position "cheating," can also be a useful tactic, though less so than in singles, where, again, speed deliveries realize a bigger payoff.

While related, in some degree, to the specific objectives of the particular kind of delivery he is trying to make, the positions the doubles server may take behind his base line are restricted by the position his partner may take in the forecourt before the play starts.

If his partner takes the customary stance, the server's best position behind the base line, as shown in Figure 8, is about halfway between H and J for delivery into the right service court 1X and halfway between H and G for delivery into the left service court 2X. This places him nearest the position on his own side of his forecourt toward which he will want to advance after the delivery has been made. It also requires him to travel the least distance laterally in any one direction to reach the server's return. Actually, the nearer he stands to H the more his service access to the receiver's service court may be blocked by his partner's body. And the advantages of serving nearer J or G (wider target area, greater depth of deepest potential target, lower mean height of net over which he must serve to hit his opponent's service line) are significantly neutralized by the disadvantages (more distant target, more distant volleying position, more lateral distance to travel in any one direction to reach the server's return). As in singles, some modification in position is, of course, justified if, for example, the server desires to protect his backhand or feels a good way to prevent his losing too many points to good service returns is to introduce a change of pace that will interrupt the rhythm of the receiver's timing.

Occasionally, the server's partner takes a stance near the net that is opposite the receiver's partner (see Figure 9). For the most part, such a strategy is followed to counter a receiver's ability to make winning returns diagonally across court. When this occurs, both members of the serving team will be stationed on the same side of

POSITIONS OCCASIONALLY TAKEN
BY SERVING AND RECEIVING TEAMS
BEFORE AND AFTER SERVE
INTO RIGHT SERVICE COURT

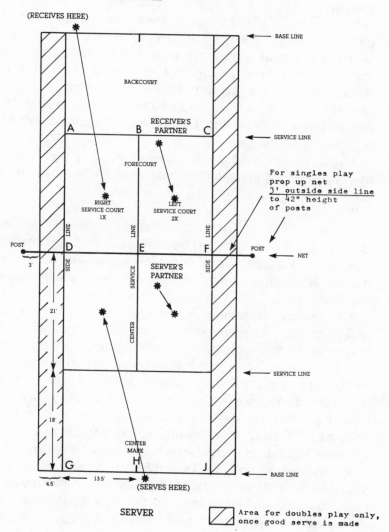

FIGURE 9

the center service line at the beginning of the point. This requires the server to stand as close as possible to H so that he is in the best position to move to defend the court on the other side of the center service line for delivery into either service court. Figure 9 shows the players' positions when this strategy is followed and the serve is aimed at the right service court—with a "reverse print" mirror image displaying these positions when the serve is aimed at the left service court. While this team formation is normally used rather sparingly, it is the one in doubles that gives the server the best opportunity to aim toward the midpoint of the receiver's service line (point B in Figure 9).

A good singles player, with an excellent serve and fine volley, may not be a very good doubles player more often than one might expect.

Why is this?

One reason may be that the speed serve is not always the bonanza in doubles that it is in singles. But this argument is not particularly persuasive. A quality server rarely has any real difficulty striking the heavily spinning, slower traveling top spin or American twist if required to do so.

A more likely explanation is that a top-notcher in singles can be so accustomed to assuming sole responsibility in individual competition that he never recognizes the importance of understanding how to play doubles and tends to overlook one very critical fact in team competition: while the success of the serve relates primarily to pressuring the receiver into making, at best, a weak return that is a setup for a winning volley, the server's partner is in position to protect half of his team's side of the net against that return and can assume a key role in eventually winning the point—particularly if he knows how the serve has been planned. A valid appreciation of this situtation calls for constant communication between players on the same team. The server furnishes the main input—true enough. But unless his partner has a reasonably good grasp of the server's target and strike intentions when facing different receivers under varying conditions, the service effort may misfire—and badly.

Expressing it another way—when a good singles player thinks he can win his serve via sheer personal talent and without the help of his partner, matters can easily get out of hand. This may be sufficient to win a number of points but is not the formula for success over the long pull.

Talk to your partner from time to time during a match. Be sure both of you know how the other plans to serve, using prearranged signals from the server to his partner during the lull between points, if this proves helpful.

Don't be bashful about holding a short huddle in the middle of a game if the situation suggests a change in strategy.

And, as a minimum, take advantage of the opportunity to discuss service tactics with him when the two teams exchange courts.

21 The Serve: Tactical Maneuvers

While there are a number of tactical maneuvers in tennis as a whole, more are associated with the serve than any other stroke.

There are two primary reasons for this.

First, the multifaceted character of the serve gives the player a wider choice of alternatives than that afforded other strokes. And, second, the serve starts each episode in a tennis match, affording ample leeway to devise a stratagem ahead of time, while the other strokes take place during an exchange—with fewer opportunities for the player to give much thought to the options at hand.

With the above in mind, let us briefly take a look at those several tactical maneuvers available to a server that can be the most productive:

SLOWER FIRST SERVE. If the player has been making the majority of his first serves hard, fast flat, or slice deliveries, he may find it beneficial to change signals, from time to time, and strike a somewhat slower top spin or American twist to the receiver's weak side and come into the net for a volley immediately afterward.

Since it will not always be successful, this maneuver should be employed rather selectively. But it can take advantage of a receiver's court position and make that receiver less sure he has properly set himself to make a satisfactory return.

STRONGER SECOND SERVE. It should be apparent that in most cases the server is best off if he strikes the second serve with less speed than the first. Every now and then, however, reversing the process and actually striking a second serve with increased momentum can be a winner by catching a receiver off guard—particularly when he has been stepping up to return the ball early and has had more than modest success doing so. The maneuver is a risky one but can pay off if handled judiciously.

THREE-QUARTERS SPEED DELIVERIES. If a server has been getting a rather low percentage of his first serves in play, he may find it best to increase the spin to decrease the velocity of his first serve to three-quarters speed, using the hard first serve as an exception to back off the receiver every now and then.

SECOND SERVE ADVANCE. While it is true, as pointed out in Chapter 20, that a player should advance to volley the return after all serves in a doubles match, it is also a fact, as explained in Chapter 19, that his chances of success in singles competition are greatly improved if he makes a practice of coming to the net in most cases only after his first power serves.

Every once in a while, however, it makes good sense to modify his service routine and surprise the receiver by coming to the net after breaking off a slowly traveling American twist second serve that forces the receiver to cope with a different set of options. This maneuver can be particularly effective if the receiver has been floating a good number of his returns.

SHORTER NET ADVANCE. If a receiver has been returning the ball to the server's feet when the server advances to the net, making it more difficult for the server to hit a winning volley, the server would do well to stop short of his customary volleying position, allowing the ball to bounce so that he can make a good approach shot and advance to the ideal volleying position.

CHANGING DELIVERY PATTERNS. Once a match gets under way, a good receiver will study the server to see if there is a pattern in the server's delivery that will allow the receiver to increase his chances of a service break—much like the baseball runner on first studies a pitcher to increase the runner's chances of stealing a base.

To counter this the server must do all he can to disguise his intentions by setting up a mixed bag of service types, speeds, spins, and targets that gives little hint of what is in the offing.

There are some serving maneuvers in tennis that are more oddball than tactical. They include such devices as: (1) the underhand serve that barely clears the net and can sometimes catch a receiver off guard if he stands too deep behind the base line; (2) the English twist serve, the only speed delivery struck with a reverse slice spin that can sometimes confuse a receiver because it is so rarely used.

Oddball maneuvers must be employed at rare intervals to be successful. Once they are used too often they lose their special value—surprise—and are no longer out-of-the-ordinary but just plain run-of-the-mill. Properly utilizing the elements of surprise in serving involves two considerations: (1) the risk taken by the server and (2) the stress placed on the receiver. Obviously the more risk taken by the server, the less success is likely to occur. What is less obvious but just as true is that the more stress placed on the receiver, the less severe its consequences because the receiver becomes inured to its impact. This makes it an equally good reason why the option of the unexpected should never be milked to death.

If a server plans to use an oddball maneuver, he should probably not plan to do so more than once or twice in a match—and perhaps at a time when he is trailing in the score and wonders if a change of pace could help turn things around.

It's worth a shot.

And it might work.

22 The Serve: Coping With The Milieu

In Chapter 1 it was pointed out that tennis opponents do direct battle with both the court and each other.

It will now be shown that additional constraints can get into the act from time to time—often in an inconsistent, indiscriminate fashion—that either affects both players simultaneously or one side of the court differently than the other.

To blanket these phenomena with a single term we have opted for *milieu*—a word of French descent that has come to mean both "environment" and "setting" in its English application. This makes it a particularly appropriate expression for our purpose, inasmuch as milieu, as we shall use it, actually embraces two categories of criteria: (1) the character of the visibility and weather conditions present during the play (environment); (2) the character and condition of the court, racket, and balls used during the play (setting). Both have a decided bearing on the tennis game being played— particularly the serve. With the latter in mind, let's examine how the service delivery can best cope with each category.

Environmental conditions that are less than perfect for playing can pose some real predicaments for the unwary server who doesn't stop to consider what these may do to his delivery or, if he does, what can be done to counter the problems arising as a consequence.

Poor visibility can be a real bugaboo, whether it results from too much or too little light. Undoubtedly, the worst offender at the "too much" end of the spectrum is a bright sun that shines directly into the server's eyes as they follow the lift just prior to the strike. When this occurs, the server can select one or more of several remedial actions, the most effective being to vary the height, and/or angle, and/or target for his lift by selecting the kind of serve that requires that the ball be struck at a position over his head that is not in direct line with old Sol. He should realize, however, that to avoid the sun's rays, changing his position behind the base line will help little—if any—and making a decided pivot in his stance may only complicate his ability to strike a serve in the way he has found best. And, he should never let the intensity of the rays be an excuse for lowering the height of his lift to the point where he is striking the ball with the arm bent in an unnaturally cramped position.

Another sight handicap is present when much, if not all, of the background in the receiver's court is so bright that it lacks contrast definition. When this is the situation, the receiver should try to select a target that is not in his line of sight with such a visibility limitation. If this is not possible, he should at least refrain from advancing to the net to handle the receiver's first return—a proce-dure that is also wise to follow when shade or lateness of the day has the match being played when light is at the "too little" end of the spectrum.

Sooner or later the server may have to contend with weather conditions that are less than satisfactory.

Take wind, for example. While air movement that is not too strong is unlikely to require the server to take specific remedial action, it can, if somewhat extreme, play havoc with his delivery— particularly the lift. This is especially true when the blow is shifting and swirling.

To counter gusty conditions that are really severe the player should make a special effort to get his first serve in at all costs— selecting the delivery that is easiest for him to make, lifting it into the wind to a somewhat lower height, employing a somewhat contracted swing, aiming at the middle of the receiver's service court, and leaning more toward using a lightly struck overspin serve that may bounce high and irregularly than a vigorously struck speed serve that may bounce low and less erratically and actually be easier to return. In so doing, the server should not shy away from making several practice tosses if he is not sure how he should alter the direction of his aim when there is a sudden crosswind or modify the trajectory of his delivery when the wind starts blowing in his face or at his back.

Whatever the situation, the server's success in countering strong wind conditions ties in directly with his ability to adjust to the direction of the air movement, no matter what its bearing. In other words he should learn how to use it to his advantage, rather than consider a wind blowing in a certain direction to be a bigger handicap to him than to his opponent. Some individuals never accept this concept and, more often than not, are the very ones who have the most trouble on a windy day.

Other difficulties can arise when there is a high or low air temperature combined with a high or low air humidity. Matters can be kept considerably under control, however, if the server will remember the following: on a hot, dry day the atmosphere is lighter, the air friction is less, the serve will travel faster and farther, and the server may want to lower the trajectory of his delivery; conversely, on a cold, wet day the atmosphere is heavier, the air friction is greater, the serve will travel more slowly and less far, and the server may want to raise the trajectory of his delivery.

Since player safety is the prime reason for suspending play when rain interferes, there is no reason for a contestant to be timid about suggesting a halt should the wet condition of the court pose a threat—even when a match is under the jurisdiction of an official umpire. Rain can also be ruinous to balls, gut, and wooden racket frames. It should not be a part of the milieu that need be parried during play.

When a player wins the coin toss and has the choice of serving, receiving, or selecting his side of the court for the first game, it is probably best in most situations to serve first—no matter what the environmental conditions. There are at least two reasons for doing so: (1) since any given player, unless he is completely overmatched, is more likely to win the first game if he serves than if he doesn't, it gives that player the opportunity to get off to a good start; (2) by winning his serve first, the player puts extra pressure on his opponent merely to stay even and continues to do so as long as that opponent does not manage to break the player's service.

There are several reasons for not serving first, which should be given consideration in certain circumstances: (1) if it is known, for example, that an opponent has a serve that is not his strong point or has had little time in the period before the match to practice or even warm up, the player can net a big plus if he receives first and breaks service right off the bat; (2) if, before a match begins, a player is nervous or senses his opponent is feeling fidgety, serving second may give the player, or deny his opponent, the extra time needed to adjust to the play; (3) often on slow courts like clay—where the serve is not that big a weapon—a player can elect to receive and catch an opponent off guard by making an extra effort to break serve before that opponent has managed to find his groove; and (4) when the weather is hot and/or humid, by receiving first, the player has the opportunity to towel off before each of his service games, since a change of courts will take place immediately beforehand through at least the first set.

Some feel that when the racket spin at the beginning of a match between amateurs of average ability gives a player the choice of court, he should select the side with the greater environmental advantages as far as one or more of such items as sun, background, and wind are concerned. They reason that an opponent's service can be vulnerable to a break during the first game, when he may not be sufficiently warmed up, and that the chances of losing his delivery are appreciably increased if he must contend with additional handicaps.

Granted that the preceding reasoning has grounds for support, we question whether it is valid in many, or most, cases. During pregame practice, the opponent should be able to sense what encumbrances he faces and what counteractions are in order. On the other hand, since it is customary for the contestants to change courts after the odd games—and, therefore, after the first game— the player is forced to make adjustments without any pregame practice when he serves the second game in the court with the greater environmental disadvantages. In our way of thinking, this can make the player far more vulnerable to a service break in the second game than his opponent is in the first, if both are limbered up and ready to play—as is usually the case. And it strongly suggests that the player receiving who has the choice of court should select the court with the greater environmental disadvantages, make adjustments during pregame practice and hope for a service break in the third game, when his opponent must, without any pregame practice, serve for the first time in that court. By the same token, in those not infrequent cases when his opponent has won the racket spin and chosen to receive, the player will not only serve first but have the choice of court too—and should again select the one with greater environmental disadvantages, make adjustments during pregame practice and hope for a service break in the second game, when his opponent must, without any pregame practice, serve for the first time in that court.

We would remind our readers that the above rationale is not intended to apply to matches between professionals. Accommodating to environmental difficulties simply does not offer the top-notchers sufficient challenge to warrant this kind of strategy. Further, finished players are careful to take the time necessary to warm up adequately before a match begins—a preparation to which amateurs tend to give too little attention.

Next, as part of our discussion of the setting for a match, it should be noted that there are a wide variety of substances that can be used to make a good tennis court. Each has a different effect on the bounce of a tennis ball—particularly when it is served. A flat or slice serve skids lower and more quickly on a fast court, while a top spin bounces higher, and an American twist bounces higher and farther off line on a slow court. The fastest surface is wood, with clay and clay composition the slowest, and grass, concrete and concrete composition in between.

A player does well to use the serve as an all-out attacking weapon on fast courts—advancing to the net behind the serve with some frequency. On a slower surface, however, he should exercise more caution, recognizing that the receiver will have more time to make an effective return of even the strongest service deliveries.

It should also be observed that the tools used in tennis are not only far from indestructible but undergo a slow impairment that can affect all aspects of the game—the serve in particular—that is especially severe if the player is not aware of how the consequences of these changes can be mitigated.

For one thing, racket strings loosen and eventually break. And in wet, humid areas a wooden racket can warp if not protected by racket cover and press.

For another thing, a tennis ball rarely retains the original condition of its nap for more than a dozen games or so—even less if the game is a hard-hitting affair. Some concrete court surfaces cause the ball to become more bald and, therefore, harder to control because it tends to sail. Other concrete court surfaces cause the ball to fluff up and, therefore, be harder to strike with speed because the increased size of its surface causes air friction to make its flight relatively slower. Stains from grass courts, and surface material picked up from wet clay courts, can make the ball heavier, thereby affecting both the height and angle of its bounce and the speed of its movement through the air.

These handicaps impose decided limitations on all aspects of the game. The best way to counter their effects on the serve is to think "high" or "low" in the course of raising or lowering one's sights and deciding what trajectory is proper for the service delivery. In this connection it rarely pays off if one tries to compensate by striking the ball with increased force. This may only make matters worse by inhibiting the timing and control of the player's stroke production.

So much for the constraints of the milieu.

Don't let them get you down.

When they crop up, give them a few minutes of extra thought—if possible before you step on court—and they really aren't that tough to handle.

23 The Serve: Practice

Practice won't make perfect—the well-intentioned maxim to the contrary notwithstanding. But it can produce a lot of improvement by refining, polishing, and grooving the skills an athlete should employ in serving a tennis ball. In truth, no player can ever expect to possess a reliable tennis service until he is prepared to spend a good amount of time putting his delivery together and making sure it becomes, and remains, a well-coordinated, dependable unit that automatically falls in place the great majority of the times he strikes the ball.

The first time or two an amateur player makes a real effort to determine how he should serve, he may want to prepare himself for formal instruction by reviewing the preparatory measures and running through the preliminary motions. In doing so, he may desire, first, to check the correct racket grip; squeeze and bounce a ball a few times to get his first real feel for its texture, weight, and resilience; and pick hypothetical service targets from various base line positions, while assuming a proper stance. And, second, to take racket and ball and execute, in order, the first respiration, the lean, the bounce, the fingering of the ball, and the recovery.

Next, he should proceed to practice the propelling actions themselves. First, he lays aside racket and ball and executes the purely physical movements of the second respiration, the lift, the swing/strike/swing, the stride, and the finish. And, second, he repeats the same actions with ball only, noting when he does so that if properly lifted the ball should land inside the base line—if a taller player, as much as several feet. Later on should any server find he is having difficulty with specific portions of the service delivery, he should revert to this second exercise, keeping in mind, however, that lifting the ball without maintaining proper body balance by performing parallel body propelling actions can do more harm than good in correctly grooving the lift's height and direction.

Once the rhythm of the service delivery begins to fall in place, the amateur can start actually serving the ball, combining the preliminary motions and propelling actions into an integrated whole, while experimenting with different combinations of target, base line position, stance, lift, swing/strike/swing, stride, and finish—the kind of session he must pursue, as need dictates, throughout his tennis career if he expects to serve with any kind of success. There are several things a player can do which could help him realize maximum results from this kind of practice.

First of all, unless he is taking a tennis lesson, he may find it preferable to practice alone, spending as much time as he feels is desirable on one or more of the fifteen steps—or parts of same. This can be difficult to accomplish if there is someone retrieving balls on the other side of the net who may give the impression that he expects the player to strike balls more frequently or, perhaps, even let the shagger practice for a while—often just about the time the player is on the point of slowly ironing out a delivery action kink he is intent on correcting.

Second, when practicing, the player should try to locate a court whose perimeter is fenced in on at least three sides. With this kind of setup, the player will always have at least one service court on each side of the net where served balls clearing the net will tend to congregate in a single corner for easy recovery.

Third, the player should maintain an ample supply of good balls for practice use.

Fourth, the player would do well to bring along some means for checking the height of the net in the court where he intends to practice. If properly hung, the net should measure thirty-six inches at the center and forty-two inches at both end positions—each thirty-six inches outside one or the other of the side lines of the court to be used (see Figure 3). Occasionally it will be discovered that someone has improperly elevated a sagging cable to raise the net at its center, an adjustment that throws the slope of the overall height completely out of kilter. Should this be the case, the player should either rectify the situation or find another court.

Fifth, the player should treat his racket arm with the same care a baseball pitcher gives his pitching arm, starting off serving slowly, increasing the speed of delivery gradually, taking plenty of rest between services, and calling a halt long before the arm really begins to tire. One good way this can be controlled is to stick to a routine like the following: (1) place the practice balls on the ground in a corner behind the backcourt where rear and side fences meet; (2) pick up two balls and take the desired stance behind the base line; (3) serve the balls into an opposite service court behind which there is, again, a backcourt where rear and side fences meet, retrieving and re-serving any balls that fail to clear the net; (4) pick up two more balls and repeat the process until it is felt sufficient balls have been served into this same court; (5) change net sides and collect the served balls in the fenced corner of the area behind the service court into which the serves had just been directed; (6) serve all of these balls in the same way again, this time into the right (or left) service court directly across the net from the one used as a target before the change of net sides took place; (7) repeat the entire cycle as many times as desirable. If followed closely, this course of action should introduce sufficient delay in the service proceedings to keep the pace of this practice activity from being overly enervating. Each individual will, of course, have a different limit, but most players will probably want to confine their service strikes to something between 75 and 125 deliveries for any one session.

In Chapter 7 we made a point of emphasizing the importance of decision making in serving, i.e., thinking through in advance what you intend to do and then actually trying to do it.

The best way to develop the habit of planning each service delivery is to follow the same regimen in practice. Don't think of such a session as nothing more than a loosening-up exercise. On the contrary, regard it, among other things, as a means for establishing and maintaining an essential behavior pattern that sees you executing a preselected series of physical motions in the same way every time you serve.

Once this discipline becomes second nature, the benefits can be very rewarding.

24 Tennis: Choosing a Racket

The tennis server must have a good racket to execute an effective delivery.

But—more important—the tennis player must have a good racket to pursue a strong, all-around game.

With this in mind, we've made the subject of racket selection for serving subordinate to our discussion of racket selection for tennis as a whole—the way it should be anyway. Further, by placing the discussion at the end of the book, we've managed some semblance of balance in the organization of our material by giving the first and last chapters "tennis" headings—an inadvertent admission on our part, perhaps, that the game itself, after all, brackets the true ultimate.

Choosing the right racket can be a headache for a beginner. He is not sure what he wants or even what he is looking for. If he has friends who have been playing the game for some time, would like to see him get off on the right foot, and are collectively able to let him experiment with a variety of rackets when he is first learning, he should, within reason, take full advantage of such kindness. Or, if this sort of help is available, he should try to locate a tennis shop that keeps a supply of demonstration rackets as loaners—sometimes for a modest rental charge. In any case, he should hold off purchasing his own racket until he has sought and received the advice of a qualified tennis professional and possesses a feel for the combination of specifications that seem best for his personal use.

Whatever the circumstances, the novice, as a rule, should never start off with a cheap racket when he does purchase one, i.e., he should make a quality buy at the outset. With rackets varying in price from less than $10 to over $300 each, this does not necessarily mean he should procure the top of the line. But it does suggest making a selection that is, at least, in the $25 to $50 range. One of the built-in beauties of tennis is that it is not an expensive sport. Going first-class right at the beginning will probably not be that tough on the pocketbook.

There are several matters that should be considered carefully when weighing the pros and cons of picking one racket over another. Let's look at each of them briefly.

SIZE. In the last decade or so, more and more players have been using tennis rackets whose frame measurements are considerably bigger than those of the average *standard* racket. Whether it is best to select one of these larger rackets is entirely a matter of personal choice. Our suggestion: try several with different dimensions before making a decision.

CONSTRUCTION. Rackets are made from a number of materials: wood, steel, aluminum, fiberglass, graphite, alloys, composites, and laminations of alternating materials—to name a few. No one is necessarily more flexible than another (meaning it can generate more speed) or stiffer than another (meaning it can supply better control). In deciding what will fit his needs, a player may be helped if he remembers that a wooden racket will deteriorate in time, a racket made of metal or manufactured material can last for an indefinite period and a 100 percent graphite racket will never suffer the fatigue that can pull it out of shape.

WEIGHT. A general guideline would indicate that men lean toward rackets that are thirteen ounces or more in total weight; women, thirteen ounces or less. This includes the stringing, which usually weighs between slightly less and slightly more than three-quarters of an ounce. In making a final reckoning of the weight that seems most desirable, consider a wide range of alternatives. If no other measuring device is available at a shop where a purchase is contemplated, take along a lightweight postal scale of the kind sold for a song in many drug stores. While not really accurate enough to measure actual weights, the scale can clearly discriminate between the relative weights of different rackets. It is particularly helpful if the player is inclined toward selecting a wooden racket, where the organic composition of the material can see the ounce measurements of several rackets of the same brand vary appreciably, despite being identified as falling in the same weight classification.

HANDLE. A general guideline would indicate that men are more likely to select rackets with handles that are 4½ inches or more in circumference—women, 4½ inches or less. Many beginners fail to give handle size the consideration it deserves. This can cause a great deal of dissatisfaction if overlooked. While the dimension is marked on most rackets, it's a good idea to take along a cloth tape when a purchase is to be made—primarily to determine the relative handle girth of different rackets, many of which can deviate measurably from the size shown.

Occasionally, a first buyer will purchase a racket whose handle girth measurements are too small to keep the racket from turning in his hand when the ball is hit off center. And, unfortunately, those who do rarely remedy matters by wrapping their handles with extra tape. In the final reckoning, the player has probably selected a good handle fit if he has no trouble gripping the racket so the fingers are positioned in the manner prescribed in Chapter 5.

STRINGING. The stringing of a racket requires the player to tackle three questions: (1) who should do the stringing? (2) what kind of strings should be used? (3) how tight should the racket be strung?

Answers to the first two questions should relate to the suggestion we made earlier in the chapter: go first-class.

This means, for one thing, that the player should get the stringing done by a recognized expert—which may or may not be someone at the place where he happens to make the racket purchase. Actually, it's best if the buyer can locate a tennis shop employing a skilled stringer in addition to maintaining a choice racket inventory. Taking a little more time to locate this combination is well worthwhile, since it's not too much to expect that even a reliable stringer may unconsciously make an extra effort to do a particularly good job if he is also connected with the sale.

It also means that if he doesn't want to go the whole way and have his racket strung with the very best material—a high-grade gut—the player should at least insist that a high-quality nylon be used. Before making such a choice, however—and cutting his stringing bill almost in half—he should be fully aware that even when one foregoes this kind of savings, the advantages of gut can be quite substantial, all things considered. First, it has greater elasticity and better recoil; second, it gives the player more control of a stroked ball because its superior resiliency permits the strings to put more drag on the ball at contact; third, if the racket receives good care, it can provide better action for a longer period of time—even in steel rackets, where its reputation has suffered unfairly because many individuals do not know how to string a steel racket with gut in the proper way. It is not durable or waterproof, however, like nylon—notwithstanding advertising contentions to the contrary that support some valiant but unsuccessful attempts that have been made to give gut strings a protective spray covering that lasts. And it eventually loses tension and can break quite readily.

The choice of strings not only involves choice of material but choice of gauge, i.e., the dimension that measures the string's diameter. Normally there are six sizes available, ranging from the heavy fifteen (thickest) to the light sixteen (thinnest). Unless he is a real pro and prepared to do a lot of restringing, the player should stick to the fifteen series—particularly if he selects gut for a metal frame.

As for the answer to the third question, the tension to which the strings should be stretched must once again be a matter of personal choice. The range in pounds usually varies from as low as the fifties (John McEnroe's preference) to as high as the eighties (Bjorn Borg's preference). And the desirability of more tension increases, as a rule, as the size of the racket increases.

BALANCE. Every tennis racket has a point of balance—or center of gravity—on the throat. And, with the exception of wooden rackets, that point on most current models is approximately the same distance from each end.

While the *teetering* spot for equally long wooden rackets will rarely vary more than a fraction of an inch one way or the other, most people have little trouble identifying the racket that seems lighter (or heavier) in the head (or handle). While not quite as vital, perhaps, as other factors, here is a variable to which a player may want to give some special attention if other yeas and nays make a final racket choice a toss-up. In this connection, when testing the balance of an empty frame, the prospective buyer should remember to compensate for the weight of the strings by slipping over the broadest dimension of the head a special three-quarters ounce device consisting of a small weight attached to a wide rubber band—a contrivance found in any good tennis shop.

In addition to the above considerations, there are other racket specification matters of which the player should at least be aware—even though they are more likely to produce a psychic effect on the final racket choice than a substantial one.

For one thing, wooden frames are oval-shaped while many metal frames are almost round. For another, the throats of wooden rackets are closed in almost all cases, while the throats of many metal rackets are open.

Finally, there are the ultrasophisticated measurements of racket flexibility (the long axis bending of the frame when the ball is struck correctly) and racket torque (the long axis twisting of the frame when the ball is struck either incorrectly or with intentional spin). These are popular subjects for analysis by tennis dynamists who have conducted extensive laboratory tests and quantitated the results in great detail, but done little in the way of clarifying how a player is expected to apply their somewhat inconclusive statistics in making a racket selection.

All of these latter variations are tangible enough—certainly—but do not merit any concrete concern because their significance cannot be easily translated into meaningful judgments. The prospective buyer will have enough to do weighing the differences he does feel and understand. If, in the end, he simply does not like a particular racket for no other than aesthetic reasons, let him, by all means, buy another. Tennis is, after all, a mental game to a large degree. Consequently, the tennis player should never ask himself to use a racket that doesn't suit him—even though the reason may be purely a subconscious phenomenon of the imagination. With the large number of fine rackets on the market today, this need never pose a serious impasse.

Occasionally an individual who has played the game for some time feels that the tennis racket he likes best for serves and overheads is not the one he likes best for ground strokes. When this occurs, he should do all he can to rationalize the matter and recognize that this kind of refinement in his thinking is not only impractical but also very probably more imaginary than realistic.

Should he still insist, however, in the final analysis, that there is a substantial difference, we suggest he pick the racket he prefers for ground strokes—the ones he will make the most often in a tennis match. Despite the importance of the serve, it is highly adjustable and, hence, more readily adaptable to various rackets than the other strokes in a player's repertoire.

And fortunate it is that the serve is so flexible, because at this stage, the reader must be aware that the tennis service is a most variegated stroke—a truth not manifest to a number of people. Considering the many alternatives open to the player—the several targets in the opponent's court at which to aim the ball, positions to take behind the base line to make the delivery, stances to assume to make the delivery, directions in which to lift the ball, ways of winding up to strike the ball, ways of striking the ball, and ways of positioning oneself to receive the return of service—you have, conservatively, well over a hundred options from which to select to make a productive service delivery. On the other side of the coin, there are comparatively few choices open to the player when he is making a ground stroke, volley, lob, or overhead.

If some would require a justification for what may appear to be an overabundance of emphasis on our part with reference to the serve, there it is.

No stroke can do more for your game.

Give it special attention.

Believe me, it's the best investment tennis can offer.

But keep this in mind, too: a server's interpretation of what he *thinks* he is doing can be quite different from what he is *actually* doing, and only a qualified tennis instructor may be in a position to straighten him out.

Postscript

Having directed so much attention to the postulate that serving is the key skill in successful tennis play, we may sound something less than convincing when we wind up stating that the greatest drawback in tennis can be the fact that the service delivery is so overwhelmingly dominant.

But this, indeed, is a distinct possibility.

Time and again, the persistent pattern of "big serve, defensive return" reduces a tennis set to an exchange of service game victories resulting in a 6–6 score and a final resolution via a tie-breaker—where, again, the serve is paramount in determining the eventual winner. In other words, while the adage that "you can never lose if you win all of your service games" is no longer a fact, successfully defending against service breaks still makes it hard for you to be beaten.

What, if anything, can be done to give the game more balance between offense and defense? The question has been asked innumerable times. And several suggestions have been offered—some that at least merit consideration, others that are interesting but basically impractical, and still others that seem rather unfeasible and are merely mentioned in passing.

Perhaps the most provocative suggestion would require the player to strike serves as now but from behind a marked line some three feet in back of his base line, i.e., the distance of approximately one stride. Such a restriction would make it more difficult for the player to: (1) realize as much success from a power serve because it would be delivered a greater distance with less speed, as well as bounce with less ricochet, and (2) reach a position near the net for a strong volley of the service return. A modification of this proposal—with similar objectives but slightly less severe consequences as far as the service act is concerned—would require the player to strike serves as now but, for alternate points, on the side line side of one or the other of two base line marks, each of which would be some seven feet to the right or left of the center mark. This would discourage the server from advancing to the net because he would also be forced to move laterally to protect against a receiver's return in the area adjacent to the server's far side line.

Diminishing the size of the service court is another reasonable sounding method for limiting the serve's effectiveness. This could be accomplished in one, or both, of two ways: (1) narrowing the service court's width and curtailing the number of service aces because the receiver would have a narrower target to defend, or (2) shortening the service court's length and making it more difficult for the server to get as many fast flat or slice serves in play. If either of these changes were made, the rest of the present service court area would simply be called part of the forecourt.

Another suggestion would be to deny each player the option of advancing to the net until a return lands in his forecourt. It is an interesting suggestion with only one possible drawback: will the location of shots close to or on the service line be more difficult to determine if neither player is in a good position to make the call?

Dispensing with the second serve is certainly another straightforward way to shackle the service action—primarily because it forces the server to strike the ball with less pace, knowing that he will lose the point if it fails to end up in play. Since this is the kind of restraint that would substantially alter the very essence of the game's tactics, however, we have serious reservations about it being a palatable antidote.

Still another suggestion that seemed, at first, to have possibilities would prohibit the player from volleying the return of his service—thus denying him the opportunity to take full advantage of a net position for his first *post-serve* stroke. This has actually been tried and discarded because the receiver soon learned to turn the tables by making his first return a deep *balloon ball* floater and coming into the net himself. Prohibiting the server from advancing as far as his service line until the receiver has contacted the ball with his first return could also deny the server the best net position for his first post-serve stroke. But a curb of this kind might, again, be hard to monitor—even with officials—and could cause appreciable controversy.

Some of the suggestions that have been made are hard pressed to claim much if any value at all. Changing the tennis ball's standard specifications to make it less lively would do little to counter the relatively more potent dynamics of the service action but merely slow up the whole game. And raising the net would produce the same general results, i.e., it would handicap ground strokes and volleys almost as severely as the serve itself.

No game exists that cannot accommodate some alterations—tennis included. Further, when innovations are introduced, they are usually for the best because they have received considerable thought before being accepted.

Whether, indeed, the serve plays too large a role in tennis as it is played today is a moot point that will continue to be debated pro and con as long as the question remains unanswered to the satisfaction of all interested parties. One thing is certain: spectators could enjoy longer exchanges in play between top men pros if some sort of governor were placed on the service act that would invite the development of alternate offensive strategies.

It might be worth a try.

But come what may, the game is a pretty good one the way it is.

And even if at a future date some changes are made—no matter what they be—it behooves the best and worst players among us to continue doing everything possible to serve as well as the optimum combination of physical prowess and court intelligence will permit.